Cambridge Elements ≡

Elements in Language, Gender and Sexuality
edited by
Helen Sauntson
York St John University
Holly R. Cashman
University of New Hampshire

LGBTQ+ AND FEMINIST DIGITAL ACTIVISM

A Linguistic Perspective

Angela Zottola
University of Turin

CAMBRIDGE
UNIVERSITY PRESS

Shaftesbury Road, Cambridge CB2 8EA, United Kingdom

One Liberty Plaza, 20th Floor, New York, NY 10006, USA

477 Williamstown Road, Port Melbourne, VIC 3207, Australia

314–321, 3rd Floor, Plot 3, Splendor Forum, Jasola District Centre,
New Delhi – 110025, India

103 Penang Road, #05–06/07, Visioncrest Commercial, Singapore 238467

Cambridge University Press is part of Cambridge University Press & Assessment,
a department of the University of Cambridge.

We share the University's mission to contribute to society through the pursuit of
education, learning and research at the highest international levels of excellence.

www.cambridge.org
Information on this title: www.cambridge.org/9781009507417

DOI: 10.1017/9781009122962

First published 2024

A catalogue record for this publication is available from the British Library.

ISBN 978-1-009-50741-7 Hardback
ISBN 978-1-009-11415-8 Paperback
ISSN 2634-8772 (online)
ISSN 2634-8764 (print)

LGBTQ+ and Feminist Digital Activism

A Linguistic Perspective

Elements in Language, Gender and Sexuality

DOI: 10.1017/9781009122962
First published online: May 2024

Angela Zottola
University of Turin

Author for correspondence: Angela Zottola, angela.zottola@unito.it

Abstract: This Element focuses on the linguistic and discursive practices employed by digital citizens to promote their causes on social media, that is, to engage in digital activism, drawing attention to the growing importance of this phenomenon in relation to gender identity and sexuality issues. The Element proposes that the label 'LGBTQ+ digital activism' join the already existing one, feminist digital activism, and argues that, while these have been areas of interest from sociology and communication specialists, digital activism is still to be embraced as a field of research by applied linguists. It points out a number of linguistic and discursive features that are popular among digital activists and supports this through the analysis of the use of the hashtag #wontbeerased, combining social media critical discourse analysis and corpus-assisted discourse studies. The Element suggests that further research is needed to explore how language is used to propagate and popularize emancipatory discourses online.

Keywords: LGBTQ+ digital activism, digital feminism, #wontbeerased, language practices, social media discourse analysis

ISBNs: 9781009507417 (HB), 9781009114158 (PB), 9781009122962 (OC)
ISSNs: 2634-8772 (online), 2634-8764 (print)

Contents

1 Introduction

As early as the mid twentieth century, philosophers interested in the public sphere, seen as the place in which public opinions can be formed (Habermas *et al.*, 1974), had observed how communication was taking a central role in the development of society. Jürgen Habermas (1962), for example, identified the increasing growth of commercial mass media as the reason for the transformation of the public into passive consumers. More recently, scholars ranging from Nancy Fraser (1990) with her critique of the very notion of a public sphere and her conceptualization of justice and injustice, to Catherine Squires (2016) who reflects on civic engagement and public participation, have pointed out that "contemporary civil society is in part constructed, maintained, and moved toward or away from change by mediated messages that inform the public" (Jackson *et al.*, 2020:39).

As Scholz (2010:18) suggested more than ten years ago, "since its inception, the Internet has helped to both control and empower citizens," and the mediation of communication and interaction has reached its maximum expansion in our contemporary society, a time in which every action of every day is mediated by a screen and carried out through the support of some kind of technology or internet connection. This kind of lifestyle was taken to an extreme as a consequence of the spread of the global pandemic caused by the COVID-19 virus which began in late 2019. The pandemic forced most of the population worldwide to stay in their homes and switch most, if not all, of their activities online. As a result, engagement with and participation in social and political life, which already had a very strong presence online, flourished even more, given that all types of in-person events were canceled or restricted. Additionally, Xie and Yus (2021:454) posit that the rise of the internet and the increasing advances in technology that make connectivity always available for everyone are leading to a condition in which "human beings are now living a substantial part of their lives in digital environments," and as a result we have become what one could call digital citizens (Ohler, 2010) living a digital existence (Lagerkvist, 2019).

Against this backdrop, in this Element I explore the linguistic and discursive practices employed by digital citizens (Mossberger *et al.*, 2007) to promote their causes on social media – in other words to engage in digital activism. I carry out this investigation keeping in mind "that language can not only describe the world around us but also 'do things' and evoke changes" (Chałupnik and Brookes, 2022:310). Particularly, the Element attempts to shed some light on the growing role played by this phenomenon in relation to issues concerning gender identity and sexuality. In fact, I believe that the internet provides an ideal space for marginalized groups such as those that include individuals who position themselves within the LGBTQ+ community, and thus it is well suited to exploring the power of taking emancipatory discourse (Nartey, 2022a) to the mainstream. As Nartey suggests, it is of the outmost importance to maintain the focus on members of nondominant, marginalized and disempowered groups and oppressed people, so as to "reconstruct their experiences in a manner that gives them voice, agency and a positive identity" (2022:2). The advantage of this type of research also lies in the possibility of providing the reader with valuable insights on how positive transformations can be brought about (Breeze 2011:521).

This Element includes a review of the most recent literature on digital activism (Section 2) from various fields. Whereas there are many studies which focus on the language used for more "traditional" forms of activism, even with a linguistic viewpoint (e.g., Avineri *et al.*, 2018; Hart and Kelsey, 2022), here I attempt to trace the way in which "creating a hashtag [became] the artery for organizing resistance" (Jackson *et al.*, 2020:11). This section retraces the history of digital activism, providing some definitions of this practice and also addressing some of the possible critical features of this modality of mobilization.

Kaun and Uldam (2018:2102) suggest that the wide range of disciplinary approaches to digital activism is still not all-encompassing, as it either focuses more on the digital side of the phenomenon by reflecting primarily on its technology and infrastructures of it, or specifically on activism, forgetting about the peculiarities of the digital spaces in which the protest is taking place. While the topic "has [inevitably and understandably] gained traction in recent years" (Kaun and Uldam, 2018: 2099), the literature review presented in Section 2 highlights a gap within the field of linguistics. While the way in which communication has changed following the emergence of Web 2.0 as well as the flourishing of discriminatory behavior that came with it has been studied extensively (see, among others, Balirano and Hughes, 2020; KhoshraviNik and Esposito, 2018; Kopytowska, 2017; Tagg et al., 2017), not much has been written about opposite behaviors that resist discrimination (in Web 2.0). In other fields, such as sociology, cultural studies and communication studies, digital activism has been widely discussed (Jackson *et al.*, 2020; Kaun and Uldam, 2018); this Element aims at describing the field but also is intended to serve as a platform to launch future research on the way in which language and discursive practices are employed for digital activism dedicated to giving a voice to those who are marginalized or suffer discrimination due to their gender identity or sexuality. In Section 2, the Element also discusses the already existing literature related to feminist digital activism, a label that communication and feminist scholars are already keen on using, and reports on some studies that I believe could fall within a category that I propose as LGBTQ+ digital activism.

Through the scholarship discussed in Section 2 it is possible to recognize a number of features which seem to be found across the different studies. To further discuss the linguistic and discursive strategies used in digital activism, I introduce, in Section 3, a case study that aims at investigating the extent to which these features can be found within the linguistic and discursive practices surrounding a specific hashtag. The case study illustrates the use of the hashtag #wontbeerased on Twitter[1] employed in the fight for transgender rights. This case study can be positioned within the framework of social media critical discourse studies (KhoshraviNik, 2017), an approach that focuses on the study of language and discourses produced within social media communication systems which is "socially oriented, discourse-centred, interdisciplinary" (KhoshraviNik, 2023 p. 2) and takes into account the very nature of this type of communication which is created to be used in an online environment. The case study also makes use of corpus-assisted techniques to carry out the analysis (Brookes and McEnery, 2020).

In the last part of this Element (Section 4), I aim to bring together the discussion on LGBTQ+ and feminist digital activism and make some suggestions on how to bring the field forward. Throughout the various sections that constitute this Element, it becomes clear that the web is an ideal digital platform to popularize and circulate emancipatory discourses related to gender identity and sexuality. I argue for a stronger connection, within the field of linguistics, between the current literature related to the use of hashtags on social media and the concept of digital activism. All in all, I suggest that further research is needed with a linguistic perspective, especially research focusing on the variety of semiotic systems through which meaning is created, from the linguistic system to the visual, auditory, gestural and spatial systems, as well as to the different modes within each system that might be used in languaging mobilization in online environments.

Before moving forward, it seems necessary to clarify what I mean by an activism that is more general and goes beyond the activism carried out through digital technologies. The most popular definition of the term activism, as it appears in various dictionaries, has to do with engaging in direct or noticeable activities, such as demonstrations or protests, in order to achieve a specific goal, generally political or social. This is the broad idea which guides me in defining what can be considered as activism and what cannot. In addition to this, in line

---

[1] When the first draft of this Element was written (2022), the social media platform currently known as X was still called Twitter, it was free to use and specific agreements were in place to collect data for academic/research purposes. In this Element, references to this platform are made bearing in mind its original features, and so for this reason I preserve the use of the previous name of the platform.

with ideas put forward by Nartey (2023) and mentioned earlier in this section, I choose to focus on the type of activism that empowers and creates spaces for marginalized, nondominant, underrepresented and discriminated-against groups. Certainly, those who argue in favor of more divisive and conservative views of society could say that their actions can also be included within the digital activism label, and the various discussions about free speech that gravitate around these ideologies sometimes make it hard to contest this assertion. Yet, in this Element, I leave out hate-based campaigns and actions and opt to give space to those efforts that challenge oppressive power structures and genuinely try to fight for the equality of each and every human being.

2 Current Trends in the Academic Literature on Digital Activism

2.1 Digital Activism: History and Contextualization

2.1.1 Labels and Definitions

Digital activism, also referred to as *clicktivism* and *hashtag activism*, has become increasingly popular especially with online communication gaining a central role in our society. The term *hashtag activism* was first observed in 2011 in a news article, and was used to describe the increasing use of instances of activism that employed by a hashtag (Goswami, 2018). Jackson *et al.* (2020:38–39) posit "that this online activism leads to material effects in the digital and physical sphere," so for this reason it deserves to be recognized with a status of its own and to be given as much value as more traditional forms of mobilization. It is also notable that while the label *clicktivism* derives from an action, clicking, that is generally associated with the use of the computer, *hashtag activism* delimits the scope of this practice to the use of the hashtag symbol (#). Both these labels, used as synonyms of digital activism, are constraining, as will become evident in the following paragraphs.

Scholars interested in digital activism have yet to agree upon an exact definition of this phenomenon, as thoroughly discussed by Castillo-Esparcia et al. (2023). Nonetheless, the scholars seem to align with Özkula's (2021) view which suggests that digital activism should be considered "on the basis of its practices and not as a phenomenon originating from its relations with a specific technology" (Castillo-Esparcia et al., 2023). In truth, the variety of labels attached to this practice hints at the fact that the descriptor "digital activism" should be considered more as an umbrella term, given that this label does not only apply to activism done through the use of contemporary social media or computers, but more generally, it can be extended to activism done through all types of technological devices, from mobile phones to social networking sites.

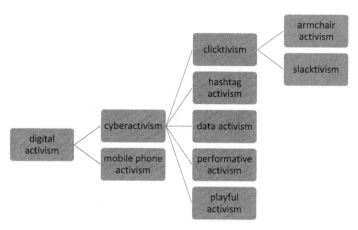

Figure 1 Labels related to digital activism.

Figure 1 tries to summarize the different labels that are discussed in this section. In addition to using online and open-source applications specifically dedicated to activism, a large number of digital activists rely on already existing commercial platforms like Facebook, Twitter, Blogger and YouTube (Joyce, 2010: 3–4), and more recently applications like WhatsApp, Instagram, TikTok or Snapchat. Early scholarship reflecting on the role of the internet in social movements focused on a variety of different types of production infrastructures such as bulletin boards, email, listservs, websites and electronic forums, that today might seem obsolete, or even be unknown by a big part of society. These, in fact, were the preferred platforms used by the first mobilizations that utilized an online platform, like the Zapatistas or the World Trade Organization protesters in Seattle (Jackson, 2018:7), as will be discussed in more detail later in this section. As a point in fact, Jackson (2018:8) posits that digital activism "does not and cannot exist in a bubble but rather responds to the larger media and activist ecologies of specific historical and technological moments." Among the variety of digital activism instances, some have been explored in more detail than others. Mobile phone activism (Cullum, 2010), for example, due to the privacy of the technology, presents several ethical impediments that make it a difficult domain for analysis from a linguist's perspective. One among the many difficulties is the unwillingness of the users to provide the researcher with a sample of the – often very private – conversations. Similarly, ethical issues can be encountered in synchronous video-mediated oral conversations, such as Skype or Facetime calls, or the more recently popular Zoom and Teams calls. This type of data should not be collected without the users' agreement and knowledge of the research purposes (Xie and Yus, 2021: 457). This adds a further layer of complication to the data collection, as the researcher might need to rely directly on the participants for the collection (for example, if the researcher cannot join the meeting themselves and the participants have to take on the responsibility of recording and passing on the registration).

In line with the idea that activism online can be done in a variety of ways, Joyce (2010) proposes "digital activism" as the most exhaustive and inclusive definition for this type of practice. This label can be seen as such because it not only includes an array of infrastructures or environments in which digital activism can take place, but also different means by which activism is carried out in the digital world. Another label that is frequently used as a synonym of digital activism, for example, is cyberactivism, which, by only referring to activism done on the internet, excludes the use of SMS (acronym for "short message service," which sends messages by mobile phone without using an internet connection) or other instant messaging platforms.

The definition of digital activism comes in many forms and has been attempted by several scholars. Joyce (2010) provides one that seems general enough to include all the range of activities and behaviors that can fall under the umbrella term: "digital activism are 'practices' – habitual activities that occur within a particular context and have certain effects" (Joyce, 2010:2). To be noted here is the choice of words made by Joyce in defining digital activism as a series of practices. Joyce (2010), in fact, suggests that this definition can include a variety of different behaviors: it can be activists' campaigns with a social or political goal; it can be the spread of news stories that contain updates, images, or videos of an ongoing in-presence protest; or it can be the personal experience of joining or supporting someone else's campaign via social media or other platforms. Another attempt at defining digital activism can be found in the scholarship of Athina Karatzogianni (2015:1) who describes digital activism as "political participation, activities and protests organized in digital networks beyond representational politics." All in all, scholars seem to agree that there are two fundamental aspects to digital activism; one, that these actions must be oriented toward some sort of political or social change; and two, that they need to be mediated by some kind of technology. Technology and social change are also at the core of the notion of data activism, a label suggested by Milan and Van-der-Velden (2016), which also falls under the overarching definition of digital activism. Here we can identify two different approaches: on the one hand, the implementation of practices of resistance that contrast control by the government or by corporations through the use of data (see, for example, Kaun and Trerè, 2020); and on the other, the use of data employed to achieve social justice (the Cambridge Analytics scandal [Bennett and Lyon, 2019] is a good example of this second approach).

While digital activism has been largely valued positively for its potential to reach a much wider audience and provide a space to marginalized groups who find it hard to voice their needs and concerns, a few labels related to this practice hint at a negative characterization. Rather than viewing digital activism as a way to use hashtags to create social change, people who engage in digital activism have also been identified as "slacktivists" or "armchair activists." This has to do with the degree of agency that activists have when engaging in activism and how this activity is still very much associated with more active, hands-on, or factual actions. The different degrees also account for considerably diverse agency on the part of the activist. From a more passive way of being an activist, such as changing a profile picture to black or adding a banner over it, to using digital technologies to regularly campaign for given issues (see, for example, Twitter campaigns by major associations such as Stonewall, or others, such as Mermaids, that have more recently moved to TikTok),[2] to enabling mobilization of activists such as the World Trade Organization protesters in Seattle. These are three examples of different types of activism that involve a different level of engagement and therefore agency, and that are each valid in their own way. Nonetheless, despite the validity of each individual's choice of action and the great difference between each of the types of activism just described, digital activism, at times, has been regarded as a less valid form of activism or put erroneously in competition with its live/on-site counterpart (Jackson *et al.*, 2020:39). Others have argued that digital activism is merely "click activism," a practice that Scholz (2010:27) has defined as "a kind of liberal catharsis during lunch break that gives participants the impression that they have done something about the issues, when, in fact, their online action has no offline effect at all." In fact, he continues, "very few who join political Facebook groups become involved in long-term political campaigns" (Scholz, 2010: 27). Contemporarily, we find in literature scholars who have argued in favor of less active forms of digital activism. Vie (2014), as a matter of fact, posits that even seemingly insignificant responses can be a form of resisting discriminatory behaviors against marginalized groups. Vie brings to the fore the example of the *Human Rights Campaign* (HRC) Marriage Equality logo – where the Facebook page logo of the organization was changed to a memetic image, shows a supportive environment, and draws awareness to important causes and should not be dismissed as a form of "slacktivism."

Despite these negative judgements, digital activism has, in the end, been recognized as a successful tool for digital mobilization, able to keep attention

---

[2] A charity based in the UK that supports trans, nonbinary and gender-diverse youth and their loved ones. Read more at https://linktr.ee/MermaidsCharity.

hIgh in relation to given issues on mainstream media, and has been considered especially effective among young activists to push change forward, whether it is through the creation of a persuasive slogan like #Transrightsarehumanrights or by simply using a powerful name such as #GeorgeFloyd (Jackson *et al.*, 2020).

The literature currently available on the intersection between the use of the internet and the development of social movements mainly stems from a variety of theoretical frameworks and methodological approaches that meet at the crossroads between the field of communication and feminist, queer, postcolonial, intersectional and critical race frameworks. The scholarship around digital activism has critically addressed how social movements have created their networks online, how the digital technology has been used to do so, by means of which infrastructure they do so and what role the internet has played in the development of social movements that question and challenge the current political status quo (Jackson, 2018:13). The essential feature that runs across all of these questions, like a *fil rouge*, is language. Without language there is no communication; however, this topic seems not yet to have found the interest of linguists.

2.1.2 History and Peculiarities of Digital Activism

Karatzogianni (2015) is one of the first authors to try and piece together the complex history of digital activism and cyberconflict, suggesting that digital activism, in the way we understand it today, is the consequence of a slow and elaborate process that predates the open software movement of the 1960s (p. 7). She identifies four major waves of digital activism which have contributed to changing the way in which digital spaces are used and acknowledged. The first wave, dating back to 1994, can be seen as a consequence of the enthusiasm brought on by the invention of the World Wide Web and the digitalization of interactions that resulted from it. This wave ended and the second one began with the events that happened on September 11, 2001, the terrorist attack on the Twin Towers in New York. This disaster changed the way we go on with our lives drastically and forever and, of course, influenced practices related to digital activism. The year 2001 marked a profound change in news coverage as well, and this was also the year in which the United States officially launched its War on Terror, with its consequent securitization and militarization processes. Cyberactivities at this point were so extensive that the Iraqi war also became known as the internet war, as the author acknowledges (p. 2). It is at this time that digital activism comes to be defined, according to Karatzogianni, as an ethnoreligious and sociopolitical cyberconflict (p. 15). Karatzogianni suggests that the third wave of digital activism developed between 2007 and 2010. This wave was particularly significant, especially in the United States, as the power of social media was seminal in the election of Barack Obama, the first African American president. Following Obama's election, a surge in the use of digital platforms for political propaganda and social discussion can be observed, up until more contemporary times, during which we witness the election, and later debacle, of Donald Trump. Both Trump's triumph and downfall have been strongly bolstered by his social media presence (Demata, 2018). The fourth and last wave identified by Karatzogianni is set between 2010 and 2014, a time when ensuing events changed the internet forever, from WikiLeaks in 2010, to the Arab Spring uprisings and the Occupy Wall Street movement in 2011. As Karatzogianni (2015:3) specifies, "the years 2011–2014 witness protests in countries as diverse as Portugal, Spain, Brazil, Turkey, Nigeria and India, to name but a few, as well as digital activism relating to feminist, LGBT, environmental and politics of food issues". This shows how the realm to which digital activism belongs starts to widen in these years and moves from being specifically political to also being cultural and social.

Karatzogianni (2015:3) posits that, since its inception in 1994, digital activism has undergone numerous transformations beyond its "symbolic and mobilizational qualities" and it is likely to enter a mainstreaming phase, that is to say, it is meant to become an "established element in the fabric of political life with no exceptional qualities, normalized and mainstreamed by governments through collaboration with corporations, the co-optation of NGOs and the resistance of new socio-political formations." In this regard, we might even be able to suggest that we have now entered a novel fifth wave of digital activism that stems from the changes that began around 2014, described earlier, and has continued until the present day. In the past few years, in which digital activism has extended its breadth to issues relating to feminism, the LGBTQ+ community, the environment and so on, the way activists perform digital activism has shifted to include a strong multimodal dimension, where videos, memes and images more generally play a predominant role and quick videos such as the ones produced on TikTok, YouTube shorts, or Instagram reels convey much of the content produced for digital activism purposes. More recently, in fact, Cervi and Marín-Lladó (2022) and Cervi and Divon (2023) have introduced a new label related to digital activism: "playful activism," carried out through microvideos produced by young cyberactivists, which, due to their ease of consumption, facilitate engagement in certain issues by even those people who had no previous interest in, or knowledge of them.

The diversity of scholarship related to digital activism is also reflected in the different ways in which the history of digital activism is interpreted. Paolo Gerbaudo (2017), for example, only identifies two waves of digital activisms.

The first one occurred in the mid 1990s, corresponding to the inception and the popularization of the Internet, which later led to the creation of several alternative news sites such as the Independent Media Center (more commonly known as Indymedia), as well as early hacker groups and laboratories. Gerbaudo suggests that the second wave coincides with the rise of the so-called Web 2.0 and the diffusion of social networking systems such as Facebook or Twitter. The rise of Indymedia has been identified as a turning point in the history of digital activism by numerous scholars. The network was inspired by Zapatista activists who struggled, in the first known attempt at digitally mediated activism, with questions of replicating, reforming, or creating new strategies to disseminate and popularize information. Against this backdrop, in our attempt to reconstruct how digital activism has developed and evolved, two questions remain unclear: (a) why the Zapatista movement plays such a central role in this discussion and (b) what exactly is Indymedia.

In retracing the historical developments of digital activism, scholarship has insisted on the pivotal role played by both the Zapatista movement and the Indymedia platform. Taking a step back, I should specify that the Zapatista movement is associated with a political and militant group in Mexico, which since the 1990s has engaged in acts of civil resistance involving mainly indigenous people. (To read more about the movement, see, among others, Inclán, 2018.) As argued by Jackson (2018), the Zapatista uprising that occurred in 1994 in Mexico was the first social movement to make significant use of the neonate web. While the type of technologies used by the Zapatistas eventually evolved (Jackson, 2018:6), the Zapatista Army of National Liberation, made up of a small group of indigenous Mexican revolutionaries, at a time when the internet was still largely unexplored territory, can still be considered one of the first groups who successfully built a network of communication which could be accessed globally and through which they disseminated and popularized their demands and their own content. Jackson (2018:6) defines this use of the web by the Zapatista movement as "an act of desperate creativity in a national and international media landscape that held up dominant neoliberal narratives that justified the North American Free Trade Agreement (which the Zapatistas saw as a form of genocide)." Along the same lines as the event previously described, Indymedia, currently an open publishing collective of activist journalists who publish mainly on political and social issues, developed as a result of the global justice protest held at the World Trade Center in Seattle in 1999. Although, after its peak in the mid-2000s, the network started to decline, it is now extended worldwide. The decline of Indymedia is mainly associated with an increase in the use of social media, which were more affordable economically and in terms of reachability and interaction by the audience.

Like Gerbaudo (2017), Papacharissi (2014) sees the unique connective action allowed by the internet, in contrast to the way in which traditional activism and collective action were theorized and organized, as the key element that brought social movements and the digital world so close together. In her theorization of digital activism, she recognizes the significance of individual and personal commitment in the era of digital politics and insists on the relevance of affect and storytelling in this new time in which social movements have lost their traditional lineal and hierarchical structure (p. 131). In fact, she argues that activism, as a form of personal politics, can no longer be built on rationality but needs to consider sentiment and authenticity. This can be achieved by embedding in the narrative personal and individual stories, turning the political narratives into affective narratives that today have the power to move people. This idea is also reinforced by Fenton (2016a), who recognizes the strong value of affect in contemporary discourses of contestation. However, Fenton is critical of this affective component, as she warns that mobilizations are losing their political focus and thus might no longer be as effective in producing social change (Fenton, 2016b). Fenton (2016a:162) also insists on the role of digital technologies in mobilization, suggesting that these serve mainstream capitalistic and commercializing goals, distracting from the real aim of activism, which is social change. In other words, the various digital platforms used for digital activism have the liability of simply mirroring what is currently in fashion and are at risk of taking attention away from the main goal and consequently devaluing it, as one topic can easily be laid aside to make room for the next more popular or trending issue.

One final aspect worth reflecting upon is related to the four elements identified by Joyce (2010:6) within digital activism: infrastructure, economic, social and political. These are all fundamental aspects of online mobilization and all influence one another and strictly relate to accessibility. I argue in this section that one of the strongest features of digital activism is that it allows for anyone in any part of the world to participate in activism actions. In fairness, this is partially true; in fact, Joyce observes that eventually the "government is the ultimate source of authority in most societies and its influence on activism is similarly widespread." The author also underlines how different outcomes of digital activism are also the result of economic, social and political factors. For instance, if we think about the economic element, in richer countries where there is a better internet connection the possibility of someone taking part more actively is higher. And while I have agreed with many scholars, such as Joyce (2010:5), who posits that the nature of digital activism "does not preclude people of limited financial resources from taking part in digital activism," it is also true that people who live in economically challenged countries may not have access to an internet connection, for example, or to a technological device. In addition to this, societal norms also affect how people use digital technology for activist purposes. Consider the standards related to freedom of speech that are in place in some countries in comparison to others. Expectations associated to digital activism based on "age, gender, religion, education, ethnicity, or socioeconomic status" (p. 5) must also be taken into account. These aspects affect participation rates and access to this form of social participation.

All actions, including, above all, activism, come with their own risks. Digital mobilization might be effective for one group of activists who can communicate and organize the collective action in a way that actually favors social and political change without harming anyone, but the same cannot be said for other groups, because online traces might reveal dangerous and be used by against them by those who wish to persecute any opposition (Schultz and Jungherr, 2010: 33). Digital activists, because of the digital traces that they leave behind, can be easily identified and subject to retaliation. This last aspect adds to the list of downsides of digital activism begun in Section 2.1.1, which in my view is still not extensive enough to have a higher weight on the scale that measures the positives and the negatives of digital activism.

So far, I have argued that digital activism takes on many forms, developing across platforms and modes of participation. However, it should be noted that what is defined as hashtag activism seems to prevail in the current digital activism landscape. This could be connected to the popularity of given social media networks over others, but mostly it seems to be related to the role of the hashtag itself. The practice of employing hashtags on social media has now become so popular that it influences every aspect of our lives. In fact, we use hashtags when we want to participate in more collective actions, such as presidential elections or international protests, as opposed to more individual day-to-day activities, such as personal posts on our favorite social media platform or even communications with our friends. "While hashtags have extended the communicative reach of those who already benefit from widespread access to the public, for those individuals and collectives unattached to elite institutions, Twitter, and the unifying code of the hashtag, have allowed the direct communication of raw and immediate images, emotions, and ideas and their widespread dissemination in a way previously unknown" (Jackson *et al.*, 2020:34).

In contrast to other types of digital activism discussed in previous sections, "hashtag activism is a uniquely twenty-first-century phenomenon" (Jackson *et al.*, 2020:40) that started on Twitter and then expanded to most social networking platforms. On the one hand, Twitter recalls the affective aspect discussed earlier and observed by Papacharissi (2016): ordinary people trying to change, challenge and redefine the public debate and push social change, often putting on public display personal stories and life experiences, enabling them to come together beyond geographical distance, social status or availability. Twitter allows marginalized groups to have a voice and space to say what they have to say; and historically, social breakthroughs, especially in a country like the United States, from the abolition of slavery to LGBT+ rights, have always stemmed from alternative and marginalized networks (Jackson *et al.*, 2020: 40–41).

A number of scholars have traced in the work of Indigenous, Black and other racially or sexually marginalized groups a long-standing tradition of political critiques that have played a fundamental role in the push toward cultural and political change – work done mainly online and through extended digital networks that allow for a greater popularization and a safer space in which to spread novel ideas. One of the most recent and effective examples that led to a great movement asking for racial justice was the use of the hashtags #BlackLivesMatter and #Ferguson. These, as Jackson (2018:13) has pointed out, not only have functioned as long-existing sites in which these marginalized groups have been able to loudly challenge white supremacist violence but also have helped to infiltrate mainstream media and political debates in the United States and worldwide. An additional advantage of these protests is also related to the fact that the digital component not only allowed them to go viral in the online environments in which they were created but also fueled offline actions (Jackson, 2018:13).

2.2 Language, Gender, Sexuality and Online Mobilizations

Activism within the LGBT+ and feminist community is not a new phenomenon. On the contrary, it is thanks to the mobilization of the people, who fearlessly and tirelessly choose to be in the front lines of these fights to see basic human rights recognized for everyone regardless of gender identity or sexuality, that social change happens. These movements have been on the radar of scholars for years, exploring the way people organize themselves, how the protests are carried out and how linguistic and discursive practices impact on this type of communication.

As Jackson *et al.* (2016) point out, the technological structures of the internet have been used by individuals who identify within marginalized groups in society such as lesbian, gay, bisexual, transgender and queer activists, as much as by Black and Latino communities whose interest often lies in racial justice activism, not only to make claims of civic and social belonging, but also to build life-saving networks of support. This is true not only for social media platforms but also, for example, for the creation of other materials and spaces, as the transgender and queer communities have done on many occasions, using their understanding and experience as marginalized communities to create websites, blogs, digital zines, dictionaries, video content and cross-platform social media networks that can be positioned outside the cultural and political spaces in which their identities are disciplined and punished (Bailey, 2016; Cavalcante, 2016; Jackson *et al.*, 2017). This parallel online world in which trans and queer people are able to thrive contributes to a greater attempt at a different type of politics that aims not only at shifting the mainstream narrative but also at developing collaborative and experimental political projects (Hundley and Rodriguez, 2009; Rawson, 2014). Thanks to their function as a new paradigm of communication (KhoshraviNik, 2017), social media are a fertile ground in which change can be engendered, and therefore a particularly relevant area of analysis when it comes to the representation of gender and sexual identities. KhoshraviNik (2017:752) highlights this very aspect of social media by suggesting that it provides a new type of communicative affordance by developing at the intersection of mass and interpersonal communication.

2.2.1 Feminist Digital Activism

In an effort to narrow down the causes of online mobilization to gender identity and sexuality issues in this Element, we can say that feminist movements have been the forerunner of digital activism. The number of studies that have explored how feminist activists have brought their fights online while continuing them offline is, in fact, overwhelming. Jouët (2018) suggests that digital media not only are largely used by feminist activists but have actually contributed to the revival of this type of activism. Digital feminism over time has become an established field of research among gender studies and communication scholars.

In her study on online feminism in France, Jouët (2018:136) observes that this phenomenon is recent in France, having developed in the last ten years, and is, for obvious reasons, strictly linked to "a new generation of digitally skilled women." The study highlights how digital actions within feminist activism in France have led to the emergence of a new leadership and new organizational practices within the movement itself. At the same time, Jouët identifies a new model of carrying out this mobilization, defining it as "performative activism," where the young feminists not only are very keen on being visible but use a variety of techniques to do so, from visual elements like images and photos to YouTube videos, giving prominence to an element of multimodality that is recurrent within the studies reviewed in this section. Clark (2016), in fact, talks about feminist protests online having an "effective dramatic performance"; in other words, she sees it as a form of social drama "with all the elements of compelling storytelling" (p. 13).

Focusing on the #WhyIStayed movement, Clark (2016) builds on a wave of feminist research which in the early years of the 2010s focused on feminist hashtag activism, especially thanks to space provided by the journal *Feminist Media Studies*. Clark's study, beyond the concept of effective dramatic performance, concludes that the narrative logic of hashtag activism has the fundamental role of producing and connecting individual stories which become the fuel of protests. All in all, Clark (2016) suggests that hashtags can be seen as symbols of hope that help create networks of solidarity, foster the circulation of "revised normative interpretations of social phenomena" (p. 13), and help shape sociopolitical change and a culture that validates victims rather than blaming them.

In the studies published in those years, several main patterns emerge from those explorations of digital feminism: first, these movements are a testament to the ability of feminist activists to oppose oppressive mainstream discourses produced by the media and promoted by the economic interests of commercial power (see Clark, 2014; Meyer, 2014; Horeck, 2014). Other scholars focused on the importance of digital feminism in popularizing the discourse around violence against women and bringing to the fore the discussion that clarifies and strongly supports the fact that these are not just sporadic events, and that we should stay away from discourses of victim-blaming and be aware of the growing rape culture in which our society is swallowed (e.g., Eagle, 2015; Rentschler, 2015; Williams, 2015). Lastly, some scholars have also discussed the drawbacks of this type of activism, from hate speech and online threats that victims might receive (Cole, 2015),[3] to the possible structures of inequality that are reinforced in some parts of the world where access to technology might still be limited (Latina and Docherty, 2014). According to Jackson *et al.* (2019), it was due to the "digital labor" that raised consciousness among Twitter users and enabled the acceptance of alterative storytelling, that more recent hashtags such as #MeToo became so powerful and really made a difference in the social fight.

Beyond France, within the European scene, Spain has also been at the center of many investigations in this sense (Castillo-Esparcia et al. 2023). In her study of feminist cyberactivism, Núñez Puente (2011) explores the way in which the online presence of feminist groups actually supports and strengthens their offline work, giving agency to feminists and creating a space for a variety of positionalities. This reinforces the idea, argued by a number of scholars, that the inclusion of online modalities within activism has opened up new possibilities for the practice of feminist politics and the drive toward social change. This is mainly related to the new participatory feature of the Internet that provides a forum for marginalized and oppressed voices (Jackson, 2016; Mann, 2014; Squires, 2016).

---

[3] More recent work on this topic has been done by Esposito and Zollo (2021).

As Fischer (2016) argues, research in this direction also acknowledges the importance of the convergence between online and offline activism (Jackson, 2018). Likewise, Larrondo *et al.* (2019) explore the reaction of the feminist movement to the unfortunately popular event known as *La Manada*, in which a gang of men sexually assaulted a woman during the festival of San Fermín in Pamplona. The study reflects on the role of digital activism in helping build a higher consciousness concerning gender equality issues in Spain.

Along the lines of hashtag activism is also the study by Jones et al. (2022) on the use of the hashtag #NotAllMen. In particular, the authors focus on the most recent comeback of the hashtag during March 2021 in response to reports on the case of Sarah Everard, a 33-year-old British woman who went missing in London and was found murdered a week later. When this hashtag was used in 2014, it referred to a mass shooting in California by a man who identified as an incel (involuntary celibate). At the time, a strong critique in a feminist perspective arose against use of the hashtag because the sentence chosen to create the hashtag was perceived as hostile and prejudicial against women who spoke out about gender-based violence. In this sense, the stance was understood as focusing more on the defense of men rather than criticizing the misogynistic behaviors that lead to violence against women. However, the authors observe the way in which the hashtag is reframed during its latter rise "to resist misogynistic responses to an instance of homicidal sexual violence" (p. 3). Following Everard's murder, Twitter users began to use this hashtag not to argue that not all men are culpable of misogynist behaviors; instead, they were engaging in metadiscursive considerations of the hashtag itself. The analysis of the corpus of tweets considered in this study highlights how the reframing of the hashtag #NotAllMen expressed a largely antimisogynist stance. This was reinforced by the use of terms such as "stfu" [shut the fuck up] or "rapist," "harass," and "misogyny," used to shed light on women's condition of continued and continuous vulnerability to male violence. The authors also problematize this use of the hashtag, relying too much on hetero-normative dichotomies of men versus women and oversimplifying the representation of men, but nonetheless they conclude that it was a powerful model of digital counterprotest. Compared to the other studies discussed in this section so far, here we see the hashtag used for feminist digital activism not as the main slogan of the protest being carried out but rather as an element to convey the discussion around this issue.

More recently, Esposito and Sinatora (2021) have looked at activism carried out by Arab women. Considering that the Arab Spring movement was one of the first to rely on online technologies for the purpose of their protests, it is very interesting to zoom in on a specific group within that movement. In their study, the two scholars develop the idea of "digital mirroring," which they define as a "techno-social macro phenomenon underlying the circulation of visual digital material in women activists" (Esposito and Sinatora, 2021:2). In other words, by exploring activist and emancipatory discourses by feminist Arab activists online, they highlight how visuality plays a very important role and is one of the main features of these types of communicative acts. They highlight a sort of pattern that sees women represented through traditional stereotypes, for instance as mothers or as victims of gender-based violence. At the same time, these representations give women agency thanks to the specific choices made by the creators of these images, which put women at the forefront of the protests, depicting them as symbols of "female agency" by associating them with the character of a queen, for example. Tazi and Oumill (2020) suggest that this type of activism can be positioned within the label of fourth-wave cyber feminism in the Arab world.

Along the same lines of exploring multimodal communicative acts, Chałupnik and Brookes (2022) focus on the wave of protests that began in Poland, launched and circulated by the Polish feminist social movement *All-Poland Women's Strike* following the decision to further tighten abortion laws in Poland. The protest was carried out both in person and through the movement's Facebook page, which was originally established in 2016 when the first tightening of abortion laws was proposed in the country, becoming even more prominent in 2020. In the analysis of the posts collected for this study, the authors identify five different types of multimodal communicative acts: assertives, directives, commissives, expressives and declarations adopting Searle's (1969, 1976) taxonomy. Using these different linguistic strategies, the Polish feminist activists were able to construct the protest and delineate the boundaries between protesters and opposition (use of assertives); provide a polarized evaluation of ingroups and outgroups (use of expressives), where the ingroup is sometimes represented as a genderless body of all citizens and others as one woman specifically. The multimodal posts also express commitment to future forms of action (use of commissives) and the call to mobilize people to join the protests and present demands to the government (use of directives and declarations). All in all, multimodal language use in the mobilization around reproductive rights, constructed also to undermine the antigender ideological positioning of the major institutional powers in Poland, was instrumental to strategically manipulating the messages put forward via social media – for example, through the use of gender-inclusive language to construct the desired ingroup stances, while serving to bring the Polish people together and link them with people in other countries to fight in the battle opposing discrimination against women and undermining of their rights.

Further studies which focus on the use of hashtags also point out other common features in this type of activism. Barker-Plummer and Barker-Plummer (2017) look at the use of #YesAllWomen, indicating how these tweets often display shared common assumptions about the threat that women have to overcome while recounting similar narratives of lived experience. These strategies are necessary to counterattack the masculinist narrative that tends to diminish these attacks as not being very serious or as exceptions to the norm. Studies on digital feminism go beyond the boundaries of the western world; for example, Kim (2017) explores feminist activism in South Korea through the use of the hashtag #iamafeminist. The main feature that Kim highlights about this Twitter event is the fact that it was far from being ephemeral, allowing the protest to last in time and connect activists online and offline. Along the same lines, examples from India, like the one discussed by Losh (2014), highlight some prominent features of locally organized digital activism. Among these features, Losh suggests the practice of referencing proper names or pseudonyms, but most importantly she discussed how crucial it was for activists to play a role in moderating conversations online, steering people toward use of the right terminology and breaking the code of silence within the patriarchal and authoritarian Indian society. Digital activism instances have been retraced in the African context as well; Chiluwa (2021) explores the work done by advocacy groups in Nigeria and Ghana. Thanks to the use of online platforms, these groups can reach a vast national and international audience and, most importantly, communities that live in more rural areas and in which women are most vulnerable.

Specific downsides to online activism related to gender identity and sexuality were also pointed out. Postcolonial theorists and black feminists, in fact, suggested that a drawback of these mobilizations led by feminist groups through this novel modality in the western part of the world is that they possibly enable the reproduction of colonial ideologies of civility and saviorism (Khoja-Moolji, 2015; Loza, 2014). Baer (2016) adds to this criticism by highlighting the precarity of digital feminisms, which unfortunately, as discussed previously in this section, continues to reflect, in some cases, the patriarchal norms imposed onto body politics. Here, she refers to movements like FEMEN and SlutWalk, who do not try to dismantle what constitutes a stereotypically desirable female body, but in a way reiterate the practice of sexualizing women's bodies. Thus, "rather than participating in narratives of social progress or emancipation, these actions emphasize the process of searching for new political paradigms, languages and symbols that combat the neoliberal reduction of the political to the personal" (p. 30). Jackson (2018:14) thus argues that in this sense, digital activism faces some of the same constraints that offline activists have to overcome, the commodification of personal narratives of resistance that generally come from marginalized communities (Jackson, 2018:14).

2.2.2 LGBTQ+ Digital Activism

As the literature discussed in the previous section clearly suggests, digital environments are popular among feminist activists. This type of activism has in fact reached the point of having an established label attached to it, that of digital feminism. However, LGBTQ+ activism has not been left out of the conversation presented so far; in fact, online platforms are increasingly being used by LGBTQ+ activists. I propose it is now time to make room for a new category, that of LGBTQ + digital activism. In this section I review a few studies that are not explicitly labeled as belonging within this category but can certainly be included in it.

Starting with the trans community, who has to daily navigate the difficulties of "a world created without them in mind" (Cavalcante, 2016: 110; Zottola, 2021), this group has especially exploited and claimed online spaces to express themselves. These spaces also serve for digital activism; Jackson *et al.* (2018) explore the advocacy and community building of trans women on Twitter around the hashtag #GirlsLikeUs. This hashtag was spontaneously launched by Janet Mock, a trans activist, initially to support Jenna Talachova who was disqualified from a beauty contest for being a trans woman. Thanks to the self-organization of trans women, the hashtag became "a space for counterpublic engagement" (p. 1869) in which discussions about this oppressed and marginalized community were able to take place. The main features that the authors highlight about doing digital activism using this hashtag are of different types, some of which we are already familiar with by now, while others are peculiar to this hashtag, or even, maybe, this community of tweeters. Firstly, the conversation was mainly guided by trans activist groups or public figures, such as Mock herself but also other popular trans advocates such as Laverne Cox, Carmen Carrara and Geena Rocero. Another interesting feature of the users of this hashtag was the high level of engagement between the users, tweeting at or about one another and engaging directly with the public figures. Lastly, Jackson *et al.* (2018:1877) conclude that the women who use this hashtag mainly do it to (a) share everyday, mostly mundane, experiences, (b) advocate for trans issues, with a special focus on intersectional experiences and (c) celebrate trans women and their accomplishments. Ultimately, the discourse surrounding the use of this hashtag, following the principle of "the personal is political," aids these activists not only to fight for trans people's rights but also to normalize trans lives.

An attempt at normalizing lived experiences of LGBTQ+ people also occurred when the hashtag #GrowingUpGay was launched (Barksdale, 2015).

Following the already trending #GrowingUpBlack and #GrowingupLatino (Finley, 2015), this hashtag uses comedic trends to talk about personal narratives of people's childhood and adolescence as members of the LGBTQ+ community. Fruttaldo (2020) explores in more detail the use of this hashtag and describes it as a "bonding icon," in other words "a social emblem of belonging" (Stenglin, 2011:50, cited in Fruttaldo, 2020:286). This hashtag goes from being the instrument of humor to creating a space where people can come together and express their restlessness as members of a marginalized and discriminated group. Fruttaldo identifies several discursive patterns through which this space is constructed and this fight is externalized. One of the dominant patterns highlighted by the author is related to the narration of family experiences and shared forms of emotional connection associated with common personal struggles.

Along the lines of the multimodal feature, which has already been discussed several times so far, Jenzen and Lewin (2021) introduce the concept of LGBTQ+ visual activism, which, they argue, has developed in a fluid arena in which the visual arts merge together with popular culture and intersect with politics. In other words, they observe how young LGBTQ+ individuals resort to visual resources to advocate for cultural and social change. In line with Fenton's (2016a) proposal, Jenzen and Lewin point to how this type of digital activism at times intersects with marketing strategies and neoliberal views. In my view, this could be perceived in two different ways: as a downside, if we look at it in line with what feminist scholars have theorized and has been discussed earlier, where activism follows the same mainstream neoliberal and economic fluxes; but we could look at it the other way around, as exploiting these kinds of cultural crazes to engage with as many people as possible, even those who would not be interested in such discourses if these did not sound to them like "mermaids to Ulysses." The questions of where we draw the line, and who is exploiting whom, might never be answered.

Moving away from hashtag activism, another example that fits the discussion here is a study on the significance associated with the use of the word "rainbow" by both antigender and LGBTQ+ activists in Polish media (Baran, 2022). In this study, Baran collected more than five hundred texts from media platforms that include news outlets, activist organizations, websites and social media from both right- and left-wing political leanings to investigate the use of this word, *tęcza* in Polish, as a floating signifier (Laclau, 2005; Borba, 2022) standing for the LGBTQ+ community, to explore the extent to which the word is used by both supporters and opponents of civil rights in Poland. The study shows that this term is used positively by left-wing and liberal individuals who post on these platforms, and negatively, associating it to words like "plague," by those who are politically aligned with right-wing politics. The positive uses of the term are generally found in cases in which the discourse put forward by antigenderists is being exposed and discredited. This becomes even more relevant if we consider that, despite the fact that a similar number of texts by the two opposing sides were collected, the use of the word "rainbow" was twice as more frequent in texts collected from left-wing outlets. All in all, the author concludes that the findings of her work can be considered significant because they are a tangible example of the process through which antigenderists tried to engage in a process of resignification, through the strategy of grafting (Gal, 2018), of terms and concepts that are originally associated to the LGBTQ+ community. By using language that is generally associated to the LGBTQ+ community in their exclusionary discourses, they try to exploit these terms in their favor. However, forms of resistance are simultaneously used to respond to these attacks and endure the fight against queerphobia by continuing to adopt those same lexical choices.

One last study is worth mentioning here. Once again, as with other studies included in this literature review, this work does not fit within a linguistic theoretical and methodological approach, but nonetheless reflects how language is used for LGBTQ+ digital activism. I refer to the research carried out by Robert Phillips (2014, 2020), who takes an anthropological perspective to the diachronic analysis of LGBTQ+ movements and the way in which they conducted protests in Singapore from 1993 to 2019. The first and most important finding highlighted by Phillips is that it is thanks to LGBTQ+ movements that nonnormative sexuality and identities were finally included within the mainstream public discourse in Singapore, and he recognizes the rise of the internet as the driving force of the movement. In fact, Phillips posits that it was the relative freedom allowed by digital infrastructures that granted LGBTQ+ Singaporeans the power to connect among each other, form networks and put forward their stance as sexual minorities within Singaporean society. This research contributes to the understanding of how movements that represent discriminated and persecuted minorities in authoritarian and more conservative settings must find their own peculiar way to resist, which most likely moves away from predetermined Western knowledge on how activism should be done. In the earlier work, Phillips (2014) introduces the concept of *illiberal pragmatics* and neoliberal homonormativity. The author further discusses these two concepts in his book, *Virtual Activism* (2020), and adds the additional notion of *tongzhi* discourse. The first two ideas shed light on the ambivalent and contradictory logic used by the Singaporean authorities when dealing with LGBTQ+ issues and how LGBTQ+ people manage to adjust to mainstream discourses of power in Singapore by aligning with traditional family values, while *tongzhi* discourse introduces the view by which sexual politics can be rooted in social harmony rather than binarism. This led LGBTQ+ activists in Singapore to shift their discourses from rights-based, as we are accustomed to seeing in Western countries, to discourse that centers around the performance of homonormative identities as the key to implement resistance and strategic stance taking. To some extent, this technique seems to recall some of the strategies put forward by the trans community by which the discussion is made more personal and individualized specifically to give a name and face to those people who are being persecuted rather than leaving the discussion at a more abstract level. The discussion in Phillips's works also circles back to the question of how activism can be done in less welcoming environments and perhaps can be seen as an example of how similar results can be achieved by playing the game in a different way. Nonetheless, the role of digital environments in scenarios like the one outlined earlier remains central. Additionally, the reflection that Phillips proposes in his book (2020) seems to be peculiar within the greater discussion in this book, because it is proof of the need to look beyond the ways that seem more popular to carry out activism and more specifically digital activism. The work of Yamamura (2022) echoes these observations in discussing the relocation of social practices related to LGBTQ+ activism to the digital space within the Japanese context as a consequence of the COVID-19 pandemic. In this scenario, Yamamura observes a process of transnationalization where local Japanese LGBTQ+ activist groups sought for support and the creation of networks beyond national borders although still remaining within the boundaries of Asia, shifting away from a fundamentally Western view. One of the highlights of this way of doing LGBTQ+ digital activism in Japan is the opening of the community by switching to a bilingual communication strategy that added English as a lingua franca for communication aiming at reaching a greater audience. This also allowed the discussion to broaden to the use of inclusive terminology related to the queer world and foster awareness about gender diversity issues.

Although the most prolific one – at least until recently – Twitter is not the only cyber site at which we have witnessed LGBT+ digital activism practices. Tortajada et al. (2021) argue, in fact, that YouTube is a site for digital trans activism, where it is possible for YouTubers who identify outside the binary dichotomy to perform their "non-binary subaltern body [...] therefore visually materializing the possibility of becoming" (p. 1102), using this platform to become "media-bodies" (quoting Raun, 2010). Tortajada et al. (2021) examine the vlogs of the Spanish trans YouTuber Elsa Ruiz Cómica to analyze the extent to which a presence such as this one within the YouTube platform serves as a form of activism for the trans community. The authors argue that YouTube, together with Instagram, have become the ultimate spaces for LGBTQ+ activism where gay and trans people, mainly youth, are able to tell their stories and take their stances. In the case specifically analyzed here, the investigation points to the use of humor and irony, and often of metaphors, in order to discuss the topics of interest.

This brief section has considered some studies which can be included within the LGBTQ+ digital activism category. The brevity of the section mirrors the enormous gap that still needs to be filled in this area. A few points can be drawn from this review that can be considered relevant in moving forward. Firstly, it must be noted how, unfortunately, some relevant studies have been excluded from this review due to their distance from even a more loosely intended linguistic perspective. Nonetheless, the studies that are not considered in detail here highlight how a number of other digital platforms also play a pivotal role in LGBTQ+ digital activism (see, for example, Heuer and Macomber, 2022 and Onanuga, 2023 on the use of Instagram, and Webster, 2022 on the use of Reddit). Still, we need to acknowledge the importance of Twitter in comparison to other social media resources. The relevance of Twitter has, since its acquisition by Elon Musk and its rebranding into X, inevitably embarked on a path which presumably will change this status, as many users have chosen to migrate to other social media platforms and either shut down their Twitter account completely or use it only partially. Secondly, as I mentioned at the beginning of this section, many are the studies published on the topic of online activism within the queer community which I wish to group under the label LGBTQ+ digital activism because it is indeed what they are about, even if they are not categorized as such. In my search, I often also came across other works which did not talk about activism per se but investigated the way in which marginalized communities are, nonetheless, being cared for though other types of actions, for example by calling out people on social media for being homo-transphobic or by explicitly positioning oneself as an ally. These are also attempts to resist bigotry and hatred; in this sense, the label introduced in this Element, LGBTQ+ digital activism, opens up a space for the inclusion of these types of actions as well, as they also aim at empowering and giving spaces to marginalized and discriminated groups.

Lastly, I cannot look beyond the reason why I was able to include in this review even studies that are positioned outside the field of linguistics; that is, the centrality of language, linguistic and discursive practices within LGBTQ+ digital activism. An additional element of this last point, one that strongly takes its place within this literature review, is the multimodal component of many of the case studies discussed in this and the previous section, which becomes a predominant factor through which ideas are expressed and resistance is articulated within the digital activism realm, completing and sometimes taking over a more traditional use of semiotic resources.

The following section presents a novel case study of LGBTQ+ digital activism that is related to the lived experiences of the trans community and their fight against a type of politics which continues to threaten their very existence.

3 Case Study: #wontbeerased

3.1 Introduction and Aims

In this section, I discuss a case study that focuses on the Twitter platform and serves as an example of what can and should be labeled as a study on LGBTQ+ digital activism in linguistics. It is largely acknowledged by the scientific community that Twitter has become one of the most important technologies contributing to pushing forward pressing social issues in ways that are possibly more powerful and visible than ever before in the mainstream public sphere (Jackson *et al.*, 2020:32). As mentioned in the previous section, this trend might be on the verge of changing, but at the time in which the data in this case study was collected, this statement was definitely relevant. The importance of the Twitter platform is due mainly to its ability to spread information quickly and vastly. In fact, the narratives built around and through the use of hashtags on Twitter evolve and spread much more rapidly than they would through more traditional media channels. This aspect has elevated Twitter to being one of the "major tools for disseminating information to the public in the hope of spurring particular actions or outcomes" (Jackson *et al.*, 2020:34). From the perspective of a linguist, Twitter was for a long time a very useful platform, as it could be described as a collection of language, publicly accessible, that includes metadata, available digitally and representative of a variety of genres, languages, topics, or even personalities. It served as a place for data collection not only to analyze language use or language change in time, but to observe political developments, historical events or social behaviors, and thus was a useful source for many disciplines (Zottola, 2020a). Twitter is based on social interaction between users and can be employed to create ambient affiliation through the use of hashtags (Zappavigna, 2012).

This case study aims at highlighting some of the linguistic and discursive practices used by digital activists on Twitter in relation to a specific event that targeted the trans community. With this case study I hope to shed light on a set of patterns which could be considered beyond its scope and be associated, in more general terms, to digital activism practices related to gender identity and sexuality issues.

3.2 Background

I have so far argued in favor of this new communicative paradigm and have admired the positives of the cybersphere and its role within social change.

But it is impossible not to observe that it is this very global, immediate and participatory nature of social media communication paradigm that has also made the cybersphere a breeding ground for the expression and dissemination of a range of exclusionary, intolerant and extremist discourses, practices and beliefs (Kopytowska, 2017). This behavior seems to have been taken on not only by ordinary people, but also and especially by politicians who seem to have found in Twitter a very effective means to communicate their thoughts and political ideas, not only personally or directly but also through false accounts or bots used to push their political agenda. One in particular is former president of the United States of America Donald Trump, who has declared in an interview that in truth it is thanks to Twitter that he managed to become president (Demata, 2018). Twitter was also one of the platforms that led to the decline of the former president, who was eventually banned from it after using it as a means to direct and encourage an assault on Capitol Hill, the metonymic but also actual site of the US government, in January 2022. From the beginning of his mandate Trump repeatedly used this platform to make official communications, while also using it to attack and denigrate the LGBTQ+ community. One of the most famous examples can be traced back to July 2017, when Trump announced a major change in the regulations for military service via a tweet. The tweet was posted in July 2017, and the actual law was reinforced in August. This law banned all trans people from being in the military. Before this, after he was elected in November 2016 and began his mandate as 45th president of the United States in January 2017, he had already attacked the trans community many times: in February 2016, by acting upon the law that allowed trans students to use toilets in public school, choosing them according to their gender identity; in July 2016, when the Department of Justice filed a legal brief on behalf of the United States in the US Court of Appeals, arguing that the 1964 Civil Rights Act does not prohibit discrimination based on sexual orientation or gender identity, implying that the administration should not prohibit this discrimination either; and lastly, in December 2016 when the staff at the Centers for Disease Control and Prevention was instructed not to use words such as "transgender," "fetus" or "science-based" in any official documents. The growing disdain for transgender people that rippled across the USA and was mirrored by all of these actions led to a final move against the trans community culminating in October 2018, when the Department of Health and Human Services announced that they wanted to revise Title IX of the Federal Civil Rights law to elaborate and establish a legal definition of sex and gender identity according to which gender was a biological and immutable condition. A number of protests were raised across the country to fight this and say loud and clear that transgender people would not be erased, and a gathering organized by GLAAD[4] was held in Washington Square Park, NY, on the same day this was announced, followed by a rally in front of the White House on the next days (10/22/2018). At the same time as Twitter was being used by the President of the United States to persecute a minority, this platform became the place for a counterattack, and the hashtag #wontbeerased became the symbol of this protest. I became interested in the way this *counterattack* was put forward on Twitter and decided to analyze the linguistic and discursive practices that were being used on the social media to pursue this protest. The following sections describe the data considered for this case study and the methodology used to analyze it, and discuss the analysis.

3.3 Data and Methodology

In order to carry out this analysis, the #wontbeerased corpus was created.[5] Tweets were scraped using the Twitter API Academic Research Access tool, which allows researchers to download public tweets for free.[6] The corpus was collected on a time span that stretches between October 2018 (the first tweet included the date October 21, when the protest started) and September 2021. The search terms used to download the data are based on the hashtag in all its forms, including #wontbeerased, #WONTBEERASED and #WontBeErased. The search was limited to the English language and includes the original posts, replies and retweets. Although replies and retweets are generally left out when building a corpus of tweets, as they can be seen as adding *noise* to the data, in this case study I am interested in observing the extent to which discourses around this hashtag are spread; therefore replicates of a Tweet or replies to it contribute to understanding how the hashtag spreads and how it is employed by Twitter users. Whether the use of the hashtag is relevant to the activist actions or is used in a reply to troll activists, this is relevant to the analysis of its use and to draw conclusions on the linguistic and discursive style of digital activists. The result of this search generated a corpus of 870,116 words that equals to 40,331 different texts. Given that the corpus is made on one text type and built around a single search string, it can be defined as a specialized corpus (Koester 2022); while not extremely large, it is still *representative* (Gillings et al., 2023: 8) of the type of language that I am interested in investigating here (on adequate corpus sizes, see Egbert et al., 2022). Koester (2022) specifies that while specialized

---

[4] https://www.glaad.org.
[5] The corpus is available through the platform OLA: Open Language Access found at ola.unito.it.
[6] I would like to thank Dr. Andressa Rodrigues Gomide for her support in the creation of the corpus.

corpora are not adequate for certain types of analyses, among which are lexis and phraseology, they offer a distinct advantage to delve into contextual information and are useful for exploring in more detail the link between "the corpus and the contexts in which the texts in the corpus were produced" (p. 49).

As for the theoretical framework to which I refer to carry out this analysis, I believe the work can be positioned within the broader field of Social Media Critical Discourse Studies (KhoshraviNik, 2017). Methodologically, I add a Corpus-Assisted Discourse Studies (CADS) perspective (Gillings *et al.*, 2023; Partington *et al.*, 2013). In this sense, the tools of corpus linguistics were used here to simplify the processing of the data, while the analysis carried out can essentially be considered qualitative. Much could be said about the combination of these two approaches and the benefit that this synergy brings. I believe that this discussion is outside the scope of this Element, therefore the reader will find here a brief introduction to the two approaches. Social Media Critical Discourse Studies is a problem-oriented approach that addresses the complexities of digital discursive productions; in other words, it considers language in the way it is produced within digital technologies (KhoshraviNik, 2017; KhoshraviNik and Esposito, 2018) and how these new spaces of participatory communication influence the production and circulation of given discourses, ideas and values. The peculiarity of Social Media Critical Discourse Studies (SM-CDS) lies in the triangulation of the analyses of the processes of production, consumption and distribution of the communicative act within the cybersphere without leaving behind the impact of this communicative paradigm. Social Media Critical Discourse Studies considers power relations and how these are negotiated through dominant discourses and mainstream ideologies within social media platforms, mapping the different discourses and bearing in mind that they are shaped by technology (KhoshraviNik, 2022). Against this backdrop, the analysis in this section takes a "bottom-up" approach, which aims at identifying "recurring linguistic and rhetorical patterns in the texts included in the data set and aims to generate hypotheses *a fortiori*" (Riboni, 2020: 58). In terms of the CADS approach, I align in this work with the definition provided by Gillings *et al.* (2023) that defines CADS "as the examination of textual data, applying a corpus linguistics methodology, to explore the two-way relationship between discourse and society" (p. 5). In other words, I use this approach to automatically detect regularities (and irregularities) in the way in which words come together in tweets and try to explain how their relationship is situated within the sociocultural–political context – in the broader context of the web, to describe the extent to which discourses and representations are reproduced and shape mainstream conversations around the trans community (Gillings *et al.*, 2023; Baker, 2023). In particular, I make use of the frequency list tool, the concordance tool and the collocation tool (see, among others, Brookes and McEnery, 2020). More specifically, I started by creating a frequency list of the tokens included in my corpus for the purpose of numerically ordering them; this was useful to quickly identify the most frequent words in the corpus. Generally speaking, at the top of the list, it is common to find function words, but in many cases, it is possible to identify content words that have a predominant role in the corpus due exactly to their very high frequency, which puts them at the top of the frequency list. (More on the use of the frequency tool for discourse analysis can be read in Baker, 2023, among others.) At the same time, much can be learnt about the data by noting the words that are not very frequent or are altogether absent from one's database (Baron *et al.*, 2009). This can be seen as an initiatory exploration of the dataset that can lead to more extensive and detailed analyses that may involve statistical calculations, for example, the dispersion within the corpus of a given item. A frequency list may also highlight words that one could study more carefully using other tools of corpus linguistics. Concordances and collocation, differently from frequencies, take the analysis further by positioning a specific word within its context of use. A concordance analysis offers an in-depth overview of a given word within the corpus, providing a list of all the times it is found in the corpus, namely, its occurrences within its context of use; this word normally comes to be known as the *node word*, and in a concordance line it is presented at the center of the sentence with a few words occurring to the left and right. Concordance lines can be sorted in a variety of ways. This type of analysis is useful to highlight repeated language patterns that occur in relation to a given word or to understand the context of that word in more detail (Hunston, 2002). In particular, I used this tool to zoom in on specific elements of the corpus, for example to explore in more detail the verbal patterns reported in Section 3.7. Lastly, collocation analysis involves the statistical calculation of the association between lexical items. In other words, a collocation analysis generates a list of the most significant words which appear next to or nearby a given node word and can be defined as "the phenomenon surrounding the fact that certain words are more likely to occur in combination with other words in certain contexts" (Baker *et al.*, 2006:36). A variety of measures can be used to calculate collocations, and their choice is based on the intent of the researcher (Brezina, 2018). Collocation analysis is useful to identify the discursive patterns around the use of a given word or phrase. In contrast to concordances, which do not involve any statistical measurement and focus on the direct context of occurrence, collocations are a way to have a more general overview of broader semantic patterns associated to the word or phrase (Biber and Reppen, 2015). For the case study, I carried out a collocation analysis of the hashtag #wontbeerased.

To investigate the data, I use two different softwares: *Wmatrix* (Rayson, 2009), for an initial exploration of the main semantic domains found in the data, and *CQPweb* (Hardie, 2012), for a more detailed analysis of the language used. When data is uploaded to *Wmatrix* it is automatically tagged by CLAWS (Garside and Smith, 1997), a grammatical tagger for part-of-speech created at Lancaster University (each word is provided with information about its grammatical function) and semantically tagged by USAS (Wilson and Rayson, 1993), an English semantic tagger also created at Lancaster University. For this case study, I focused on the discourse fields generated by the second type of tagging. Simply put, each word is assigned a tag that indicates a discourse field that fits the meaning of that term, namely, "time" or "emotions." Using log-likelihood as a standard value,[7] a frequency list of the tags is created and compared against the frequency list of the tags of a reference corpus; in this case, the reference corpus used is BNCwritten sampler (Burnard, 1999), already available on *Wmatrix*, and this comparison generates a final list of the key semantic domains in my corpus.

As for *CQPweb*, the corpus was tokenized and tagged for part-of-speech using a Spacy-trained model and pipeline for English.[8] This software was used to carry out the different analyses mentioned earlier.

3.4 Hashtagging and Direct Tags

The initial exploration of the data through the use of the semantic analysis tool *Wmatrix* revealed a very specific pattern that involves the use of hashtags. Hashtagging, that is, the practice of using the symbol # in combination with words, phrases, or entire clauses as a support slogan or symbol of the issue described in the text of the tweet, or embedded within the tweet itself, is not a novel procedure; on the contrary, it is quite popular on this platform and in social media communication practices more generally. Hashtags have been defined as enabling users to embed metadata in their social media posts (Zappavigna 2018), and it has been recognized that they have gone beyond being simply useful ways to make talks searchable to devices through which people create networks, or systems of online ambient affiliation (Zappavigna 2012). However, the mode in which hashtags are used in this corpus takes their function a step forward. In fact, I argue that this can be considered as one of the main features of, and peculiar to the practices that revolve around LGBTQ+ digital activism. Differently from what we are usually used to seeing, the tweets that use the hashtag #wontbeerased have a tendency of including within the text

---

[7] To read more about log-likelihood and other statistical measures, see, among others, Evert (2008).
[8] https://spacy.io/models/en.

not only this one hashtag but a high number of other hashtags as well. This is suggested both by the semantic analysis done with *Wmatrix* and by the collocation analysis of the term #wontbererased done via *CQPweb*, where all the most significant collocates of this node word were other hashtags.

Here I discuss the analysis done with *Wmatrix*. Once the data was tagged as per the methodology explained in the previous section, a list of domains was returned. As an entry point into my data, I focused on the most significant item. At the top of the list of the most frequent domains in my data is one labeled "unmatched" (Z99 in the labels used by *Wmatrix*). This group contains all the words that the tagger did not recognize. Interestingly, all the occurrences included in this domain are hashtags and @ signs, used on Twitter to tag a specific person or account within the post. In other corpora the terms included in this domain might be irrelevant, but in the case of a corpus collected from Twitter, these become key elements.

Table 1 shows the twenty most frequent elements that were found in this domain. As mentioned earlier, these results are also confirmed by the collocation analysis of the hashtag. In that case, collocations were calculated using Mutual Information as a statistical measure.[9] Scrolling through the top 100 collocates of this term, only nine of these are not hashtags or @ signs.

An example of how these hashtags are used can be seen in the following tweets[10] (Examples 1 and 2) retrieved from the #wontbeerased corpus.

As these examples show, the hashtags make up for a great part of the tweet, and it is very common to see more than one or two hashtags used within the same tweet.

The centrality, both in terms of number of occurrences and statistical significance,[11] of this specific feature of the corpus highlights two main aspects of the way in which activists employ language on Twitter in the case of the #wontbeerased corpus, the first one being by means of the use of hashtags, taking Zappavigna's (2018) definition a step further. The combination of numerous different hashtags and their use as the primary text of the tweets is what is being done in the #wontbeerased corpus. This also allows users to launch slogans that become empowering phrases; see, for instance, Examples 11, 14, 17 and 20 in Table 1. Because Twitter only allows 280 characters per tweet (that is, since 2017;

---

[9] Mutual Information is an effect-size measure that calculates how strongly or exclusively two items are connected to each other (Brezina, 2018).

[10] Although all tweets included in the corpus under investigation are collected from open accounts, thus easily retrievable on Twitter, I choose, unless otherwise necessary, to keep the identity of the user posting the tweet anonymous for the examples displayed here. This will not apply later in the section when displaying examples from accounts of public figures.

[11] When looking at the table we must bear in mind that we are looking at a very restricted amount of data and that the statistical relevance of the domain is intended in reference to the domain as a whole rather than the statistical relevance of the occurrence of each element.

Table 1 Domain: unmatched

	word		word
1	#wontbeerased	11	#translivesmatter
2	#transgender	12	#loveislove
3	#transisbeutiful	13	#nonbinary
4	#lgbtq	14	#lovewins
5	#transrights	15	#gendertag
6	#pride	16	#thisisme
7	#wontbeerased	17	#simplerthanwords
8	@realdonaldtrump	18	#justbeyou
9	#girlslikeus	19	#itgetsbetter
10	#resist	20	#stopthehate

EXAMPLE 1 Trans Lives Matter (link to YouTube video) #translivesmatter #wontbeerased #trans #transgender #pride #pridemonth #lgbt #lgbtq #GenderDysphoria #transrightsarehumanrights #translivesstillmatter #transphobia #endtransphobia #stoptransphobia #hatersgonnahate

EXAMPLE 2 #TransRights #TransRightsAreHumanRights #HumanRights #TransIsBeautiful #NonBinary #WontBeErased #EqualityAct #ThinkOutsideTheBinary #GenderDiversity "Injustice anywhere is a threat to justice everywhere . . . Whatever affects one directly, affects all indirectly." – Martin Luther King Jr.

previous to this date, the limit was 140), the use of hashtags to support the statement being made becomes fundamental. It appears, in digital activism, that the hashtag acquires a semiotic function similar to that of an image, that is to say that meaning-making is embedded within the hashtag itself; one hashtag can carry a much wider meaning than the words that make up that hashtag would if it were standing alone. This feature of the hashtag frees the user from the need to write more and explain themselves, because that word or phrase preceded by the symbol # already *says* everything, already brings the meaning with it. The hashtag begins to work in the same way as an image, as, for example, an emoji or meme would, suggesting that online communication is becoming more and more summarized

EXAMPLE 3 TransEquality: RTRebeccaKling: I'm Rebecca Kling and I'm #transgender. Regardless of what @realDonaldTrump says, I #WontBeErased! #TransRightsAreHumanRights

and iconographic. Along the same lines, the use of direct tagging (through the @ sign)[12] becomes extremely important as it enables a sort of interaction between the politician or whomever the conversation is directed at – the main actor, and the member of the public who is using the social media to make a claim. It forces the person who is pursued by the tag to take a stance, in one way or another, that is, choosing to ignore a tag is a stance in itself. In this case, for example, as Table 1 shows, the main interlocutor is precisely Donald Trump (Table 1, Example 6). The tweet reported here (Example 3) is an illustration of this trend. Since this data was collected, Donald Trump's account has been shut down in January 2022 as a consequence of the Capitol Hill events (Gounari, 2022) and later reinstated in X in November 2022.

The practice of direct tagging, while recognized as one of the potential new features of online communication, acquires a very specific role when it comes to LGBTQ+ digital activism, as it enables the activists to take a stance and almost force their interlocutors to do the same, or at least to be publicly involved in some way. This aspect of the corpus will be discussed in more detail in Section 3.6.

All in all, from the point of view of the structure of these texts used by trans and trans-ally activists, we can conclude that one short tweet not only facilitates the users in expressing a much more complex idea that 280 characters would normally allow, but also permits an interactive communication with specific users. Both these features would not be allowed by what we can consider as traditional activism, namely, marches or sit-ins, for example.

As Jackson *et al.* (2020:33) posit:

> These users' tweets create a continuous live deluge of information. [...] Hashtags, which are discursive and user-generated, have become the default method to designate collective thoughts, ideas, arguments, and experiences that might otherwise stand alone or be quickly subsumed within the fast-paced pastiche of Twitter. Hashtags make sense of groups of tweets by creating a searchable shortcut that can link people and ideas together. Throughout this text we use hashtag activism to refer to the strategic ways counterpublic groups and their allies on Twitter employ this shortcut to make

---

[12] These occurrences have been calculated only when the @sign has this function; other occurrences of the @sign have not been considered when investigating this communicative strategy.

political contentions about identity politics that advocate for social change, identity redefinition, and political inclusion (Jackson *et al.*, 2020:33).

The exploration via *Wmatrix* also returned other domains that were relevant in the corpus, like "people" and "pronouns." However, these outcomes overlap with those returned by the collocation and concordance analysis done using *CQPweb*; for this reason I decided to leave out the discussion related to the semantic analysis and discuss in more detail the investigation aided by the use of *CQPweb*.

3.5 Multimodal Approaches to Digital Activism

Using *CQPweb*, I continued my analysis by creating a frequency list sorted by parts of speech, this choice was dictated by the high presence of hashtags and other elements which prevented the realization of a classic frequency list. By classic frequency list I mean one compiled on the basis of all the tokens that comprise the corpus; in this corpus many words were joined together in the hashtags, therefore I believe the frequency list would not be as representative of all the words used in the data. The list presented some expected results, the most frequent part of speech was that of nouns, but some less expected ones as well. For instance, the second most frequent type of words consisted of proper nouns. These were then followed by verbs, punctuation, adverbs, pronouns, determiners, adjectives and so on. Given the nature of computer-mediated communication, which resembles speech more than writing (Yates, 1996; Knight, 2015), it seemed particularly interesting to explore in more detail the frequency list of the Punctuation category, which is not usually considered a peculiarity of oral production. Approximately 11 percent of the corpus is constituted by punctuation. The tagger employed to tag the corpus before uploading it to *CQPweb* includes in the category of punctuation not only full stops, commas and exclamation marks, that is, traditional punctuation, but also emojis, a graphical device, or "a graphicon" (Herring and Dainas, 2017), used to convey meaning on contemporary social media platforms. The high frequency of these symbols found in the data suggests that this can be identified as one of the features of the language used for LGBTQ+ digital activism in my corpus. The role played by these nonlinguistic features in digitally mediated communication has recently attracted extensive interest among academics (Logi and Zappavigna, 2021). Logi and Zappavigna (2021: 3222–3223), suggesting that emojis are widely used to express emotions, convey stances and negotiate interpersonal alignments. In fact, they draw from Herring and Dainas (2017), who suggest that emojis fulfill similar roles as emoticons, graphical devices formed from ASCII characters, which have been in use since the late 1970s.

They (a) express emotions, (b) function as nonverbal signals, (c) function as tone management or indication of illocutionary force and (d) replace punctuation or structural markers (Herring and Dainas, 2017: 2185). It is important to point out some of the limitations of the use of emojis. One above all is related to the fact that different emojis are interpreted with different meanings by different people and that different viewing platforms render emojis in a variety of ways (Herring and Dainas, 2017). These small images have become so popular that by 2016 almost 50 percent of messages used in technology-mediated communication included one (Logi and Zappavigna, 2021). We can now agree that they are evolving into a language of their own; Herring and Dainas (2017, p. 2185) go as far as to suggest that they can be considered "a complete grammatical system."

Against this backdrop, interestingly enough, the most popular and straightforward emojis, those that serve the function of "tone modification" following Herring and Dainas's (2017) categorization, do not occur frequently in the corpus and show a very low and not varied presence, the most common ones being the 😀 (smile), the 😍 (heart eyes), the 😘 (kissing heart) and the 🥰 (smiling face with hearts).[13] These types of emojis are "nonverbal, paraverbal, or paralinguistic cue[s] as to how the text should be interpreted" (p. 2188), or more simply put, a way of expressing an emotion, such as the face emojis or the hearts. Beyond these, I found several other symbols that display a notably higher number of occurrences. These are listed in order of frequency in Table 2.

This feature of the data suggests a very strong iconographic element embedded within the tweet. In addition to the hashtags, whose function, I suggested, resembles that of a symbol in the way they carry meaning, here the emojis are the actual symbols being used. These seem to align in part with the function

Table 2 List of Emojis

Emoji	Name	No. of occurrences
🖊	Fountain Pen Emoji	2,562
📨	Incoming Envelope Emoji	2,552
🌈	Rainbow Emoji	974
🏳	White Flag Emoji	391
📬	Open Mailbox with Raised Flag Emoji	357
📝	Memo Emoji	343
✊	Raised fist	275
🗳	Ballot Box with Ballot	136

---

[13] Emojis in this Element used under a creative commons licence, © X Corp. Full details: Copyright 2024 X Corp and other contributors. Code licensed under the MIT Licence: http://opensource.org/licenses/MIT. Graphics licensed under CC-BY 4.0: https://creativecommons.org/licenses/by/4.0/.

described by Danesi (2016) of being adjunctive emojis; that is, they make meaning alongside language (among the ones in Table 2 we group in this category the following: ✒, 🖋, | , 📝, 📫), but also with the other function described by this author of being substitutive emojis, in this case they replace the language altogether (this category includes among the emojis described the following ones: 📩, 📬, 📝). More specifically, the tweets that used the Fountain Pen, the Incoming Envelope, the Memo and the Open Mailbox emojis are employed in particular types of tweets that invite the reader to sign a petition to be delivered to local senators, or remind people to vote, therefore, to actively engage in more practical forms of protests pointed directly at those politicians who play a role in the marginalization of the trans community or who could help end these types of abuses. The function of these emojis can recall what Herring and Dainas (2017: 2189) define as "action," "used to portray a (typically) physical action." The rainbow, fist and white flag emojis I believe can be better described not according to their pragmatic function, as earlier, but through a social semiotic approach which takes into account the interaction between the ideational (constructing the experience of the world through language), interpersonal (enacting relationships through language) and textual (organization of discourse into a coherent and cohesive text) functions of language, following the Systemic Functional Linguistics' tradition (Halliday, 1978). In this sense, I follow Zappavigna and Logi's (2022: 233) taxonomy and suggest that the rainbow, fist and white flag emojis realize the discursive semantic feature of INVOLVEMENT. That is to say that these emojis are used to express solidarity "by employing semiotic resources to encode meaning that can only be interpreted by members of a particular community" and their allies. The rainbow recalling the LGBTQ+ community, the white flag to symbolize the end of persecution and discrimination against the trans community and the fist to remind everyone to keep fighting and resisting. In a way, each of these features recalls one of the aspects of digital activism highlighted in previous sections, in which scholars suggest that digital activism is useful in keeping a connection open between online and offline mobilization practices. In this sense, the use of these emojis responds to the most basic of the speech functions, the illocutionary, the locutionary and the perlocutionary effect (Austin, 1962) that the tweet aims at having; the emojis produce literal meaning, they have a social function, and they encourage the interlocutor to take action.

Moreover, as noted in the literature review (Esposito and Sinatora, 2021), the multimodal component is deeply prominent in the tweets beyond the use of emoji. While conducting a more detailed analysis of the elements identified in the Punctuation category frequency list, through a concordance analysis that allowed the researchers to access links to each tweet, it was remarkably frequently observed that the tweets included either a photo or some kind of visual aid, a post or a video, as Examples 1, 2 and 3 in Section 3.4 also show. While this observation is purely speculative, the way the data was collected and stored does not allow one to test this hypothesis thoroughly; in line with the existent literature, it could be said that multimodality plays a unique and important role in online mobilization and in LGBTQ+ digital activism in particular.

3.6 People

In this section I look in more detail at another of the categories emerging from the frequency list sorted by parts of speech, that of Proper Nouns. This category, which I also found unexpected, includes names of people, cities, or public places. I decided to explore this category in more detail because I believe it can shed additional light on the social actors involved in my corpus and the people/ places that are included directly in the discourses surrounding #wontbeerased. In fact, the terms included in the frequency list for this category overlap in part with the discussion presented in Section 3.4, many of the proper names are preceded by @ signs. With this in mind, I sorted the frequency list to include only those terms that are premodified by the symbol @. This search returned a list that I have sorted to include only tags referring to people. Thanks to this type of selection, I was able to detect those accounts of very specific profiles among the social actors that are involved within the data of this corpus and who can be related to the cause put forward by the #wontbeerased slogan. Differently from the procedure followed in Section 3.4 where names and identities of the users were made anonymous, here, given the status of public figures that the people involved in this section of the analysis have, I did not remove personal information. Public figures choose, as part of their occupation, to make their ideas and thoughts publicly displayed; for this reason, I do not anticipate ethical conflict. Table 3 shows a list of the twenty most frequent subjects tagged in the tweets included in my corpus.

The items presented in Table 3, excluding number 5, correspond to the Twitter handle of a specific individual.[14] In the initial list that was produced by searching names preceded by the @ sign, some were related to accounts of newspapers. I decided to remove those, but on the contrary I kept the tag related to the *Human Rights Campaign* (@HRC, item 5 in Table 3). The *Human Rights Campaign* is one of the largest and most influential advocacy organizations for the LGBTQ+ community in the USA,[15] and while this handle does not belong to

---

[14] A Twitter handle is the username that appears at the end of the Twitter URL and it is unique to each user.

[15] As they claim, for more info visit https://www.hrc.org/about.

Table 3 List of the twenty most frequent people
tagged in tweets.

	Word	Frequency
1	@nygovcuomo	1,110
2	@realdonaldtrump	752
3	@senfeinstein	407
4	@senkamalaharris	392
5	@hrc	270
6	@sentedcruz	200
7	@johncornyn	199
8	@senschumer	135
9	@secazar	134
10	@meakoopa	126
11	@marcorubio	123
12	@senrickscott	121
13	@sentoomey	119
14	@senbobcasey	117
15	@gillibrandny	116
16	@senthomtillis	113
17	@senatorburr	108
18	@senrobportman	101
19	@pattymurray	96
20	@sencorygardner	94

a single individual, unlike the others included in this table, I still view this account as presenting a reality that is very different from that of a newspaper and representative of one of the voices contributing to the narrative being built around the hashtag #wontbeerased. As a matter of fact, this account massively used the hashtag during and after the actual protest. This list, which only includes the top twenty most frequent accounts tagged in the tweets, is far from being the complete one, which is much longer, including over 7,400 items. It is interesting to note how, except for item number 5, already discussed, and item number 10 that belongs to author and public figure Anthony Oliveira,[16] all the other Twitter handles identified here belong to senators of the United States and to Donald Trump, who at the time of data collection was the president. This practice suggests that the tweets included in the corpus and used by trans and trans-ally activists are far from being impersonal or generic but, on the contrary,

---

[16] https://anthonyoliveira.com/about.

Figure 2 Open Letters account

the individuals who produce these tweets make an effort to create very personal content and above all aim at bringing the discussion back to the people, at engaging directly with those who can really make change possible, who have the power to reverse the series of injustices and discrimination that the trans community must endure.

When looking at the data in more detail, I found a language pattern that was repeated very often: "I just delivered this letter from." The concordances of this sentence revealed that all the tweets containing it were posted by the same account. Figure 2 displays an example of this type of tweet.

These tweets were all posted by one specific account, the Open Letters account. This is a bot that automatically publishes copies of letters delivered to elected officials in the United States. It is connected to a free service called Resistbot[17] that allows a user to contact an official in a few small steps through the use of text messages and a chatbot. There are 4,330 tweets posted by this account in my corpus, which makes up almost 14 percent of all tweets (this equals to a similar percentage of words, 14.9%). While this is obviously not an actual person posting on Twitter, it serves the purpose of disseminating these actions, making them visible and possibly encouraging as many people as possible to follow this lead. In addition, while the posts are not created by

---

[17] https://resist.bot.

a person directly, the bots are made by people with the intention of disseminating a specific topic widely; this could be considered in itself a form of digital activism. This practice puts these politicians in a situation in which they must respond in one way or another and position themselves publicly with regard to these issues, and when a politician is being called upon directly and publicly, even not taking a stance is actually a way of taking one.

Continuing the analysis by sorting the data to exclude all tweets posted by this account that not only follow the same structure as the example provided here but also are not representative of natural language production, I found three different discursive patterns employed by the users of the hashtag #wontbeerased. First, a group of tweets I label as celebratory tweets, used to proclaim some kind of victory or achievement (as displayed in Example 4).

Second, we have reporting tweets (see Example 5); these tweets are used to condemn discrimination committed against trans individuals or the community at large. As with the previous type of tweets, it is common to find an attachment to the tweet that allows the user to find more information via a newspaper article or a video.

These types of tweets, by embedding the link to a video, become in a way multimodal; even if the nonverbal content is not directly visible, it is attached to the tweet and is an integral part of the meaning-making of the text. In this sense, these types of tweets recall the linguistic practice described in Section 2.2.1 quoting Chałupnik and Brookes (2022), who talk about multimodal communicative acts, that is, directives and declarations that serve the purpose of both providing information on the protests while also mobilizing protestors.

EXAMPLE 4 @NyGovCuomo Signs Trans Rights Bill, Conversion Therapy Ban . . .
#LoveIsLove #BornThisWay #StopTheHate #Pride #BornPerfect #WontBeErased #ItGetsBetter #LoveWins #DefyTheName
(Link to video)

EXAMPLE 5 Ben Carson (@SecretaryCarson) "Allegedly" Called Trans Women "Big Hairy Men" In Front Of HUD Staffers . . .
#Pride #WontBeErased #StopTheHate #EqualityAct #NoTransBan #LoveIsLove #TransIsBeautiful #TransLivesMatter #DefyTheName
(Link to video)

EXAMPLE 6 @realDonaldTrump @VP @GOP I am as human and worthy of a full and happy life as you or anyone else. I stand here now to tell you that I #WontBeErased #TransIsBeautiful #Transgender #MeToo #Resistance #25thAmendment #Free2BeMe

In addition to these two categories of tweets, I retrieved another type of tweets in the data. While celebratory and reporting tweets are used by a variety of different accounts, this last type of tweets (see Example 6) are used mostly by trans people to claim their rights as human beings and use the space to fight their marginalization. These tweets written by trans people who use this social media serve to bring visibility to their identity and their community as whole. I define these as agency tweets; because they permit people to position themselves, they give them a space of existence, allowing trans people to actively change the way in which they are portrayed and perceived.

Agency tweets also have the function of reminding Twitter users that it is actual human beings that are at stake when laws are suddenly changed or representations are used to undermine a person's survival. These tweets specify that while this issue is unequivocally concerned with laws and politics, it should, above all, be discussed in terms of what or whom it truly affects, that is, people's lives that are being questioned.

3.7 Hate versus Love

The literature in the field of online/computer-mediated communication has often proven that there is a tendency for users, because of the internet's new ways of communicating, to easily resort to hate speech, using unique linguistic techniques. KhoshraviNik and Esposito (2018), in particular, highlight three specific techniques that online haters employ, and these are anonymity, seen as the ability of the web to hide one's identity; physical separation, which comes as a consequence of anonymity and is intended as the practice of distancing oneself from one's online identity, resulting in lack of face-to-face interaction and acknowledgement of people's humanity; and lastly the practice of deindividuation, which consists in relying on the group, or being part of a specific ensemble by reducing self-awareness and self-visibility. The data discussed so far, on the way in which digital activists use language, suggest that activists' linguistic and discursive choices differ largely from these practices. On the contrary, these people try not to hide themselves, but make their bodies visible by posting selfies, for example, and making their stances loud and clear. A study on the perception of selfies in posts conducted by Katz and Crocker (2015) suggested that adding a selfie to a post tends to elicit comments and encourages conversations between users who are, in turn, also stimulated to post a photo. In this sense, the practice can trigger a kind of chain reaction toward online mobilization.

While the academic literature sadly overflows with studies that tackle the way in which language is used to create hate speech online (see, among others, Balirano and Hughes, 2020; Brindle, 2016; Rasulo, 2023), the last portion of analysis that I wish to discuss here goes in a different direction and discusses a way to resist hate rather than contribute to it. The analysis relies on another of the part-of-speech categories derived from the frequency list presented earlier and reinforces the idea that digital activists, to put it in a more poetic way, spread love rather than hate. The category under scrutiny here is that of verbs. The frequency breakdown function on *CQPweb* allowed me to produce a list of all the verbs used in the corpus in order of frequency. It is very common when looking at a frequency list to find in the first positions of the list a number of auxiliary verbs, as it was in this case where we found verbs such as "to be," "to have," and "to do" in a variety of forms. These were excluded for the purpose of this analysis. We are, thus, left with a list of main verbs, those whose meaning is related to actions, events and states. The top thirty most frequent are listed in Table 4.

In this list of verbs, we find a variety of different verbal processes. In order to classify these verbs, I refer to SFL's (see Section 3.5) taxonomy (Halliday, 1978). I then look at the context of use to determine the function that they carry out and the outcome of the choices made by the activists in using them. Halliday (1978) identifies six process types: material, mental, relational, verbal, behavioral and existential. Many of the items in Table 4 are material verbal processes, namely, verbs that express the process of doing something, of a physical action like stand, fight/fighting and support, join or protect. In particular these verbs recall a semantic domain that seems to be closer to violence than love, that of war language; it recalls many slogans popular in the United States related to, for example, joining the army, or remembering the veterans and soldiers who are fighting to protect the country, a type of "warspeak," as defined by Myers (2019), that permeates the United States. However, if we look in more detail at the way these verbs are used in the tweets, we find that these are actually used to encourage people not to surrender to injustice, to tell trans people that they are not alone in facing these discriminations. This discourse is supported by phrases such as "fighting for rights," "resisting erasure," "deserving to be alive and to exist," and "attack our basic human rights," which despite recalling battlefield language – namely, fighting, resisting – present a very positive discourse. An illustration of this is displayed in Example 7.

Table 4 Selected list of verbs used in the #wontbeerased corpus.

	verb		verb		verb
1	stand	11	thank	21	show
2	know	12	stop	22	define
3	erase	13	love	23	fighting
4	fight	14	vote	24	read
5	see	15	deserve	25	feel
6	support	16	go	26	remember
7	say	17	join	27	continue
8	need	18	trying	28	loved
9	exist	19	live	29	protect
10	erased	20	help	30	defining

EXAMPLE 7 When this administration spews hate, we will speak out louder. When they commit injustice against one of us, we will come together to stand stronger. When they attack our basic human rights, we will fight back harder. Transgender Americans #WontBeErased. We won't stand for it.

The verb "stand," for example, which is the one with the highest occurrences among the main verbs in the frequency list, is mostly found followed by prepositions such as by, with and up. The examples that follow are representative of the ways in which these are used in the corpus.

10) WE stand WITH the trans* community because y'all MEANS y'all! #nhpolitics #wontbeerased

11) Black trans folks matter. Intersex folks matter. Disabled trans folks matter, indigenous trans folks matter, latinx trans folks matter, immigrant trans folks matter – Every single one of us matters. We will stand up against this discrimination! #TAGUrself #wontbeerased

12) I cannot stand by as trans people are under attack. This is not about identity but about humanity. The fight for trans lives is a fight for recognition of all people's full humanity. Stop targeting trans people @realDonaldTrump #WontBeErased #TDOR18 #TransDayofRemembrance

13) To our transgender & non-binary youth, staff, friends, neighbors, & family members: we see you, we love you, and we stand by you. #wontbeerased

All these examples show how Twitter users are employing this hashtag to write messages of hope (recalling what Clark, 2016 suggests, as explained in

Section 2.2.1) and support to the trans community. This same pattern repeats with the verb to fight; examples include "We fight for our trans brothers and siblings," "fight attempts by those trying to erase the #LGBTQ Community," or "I'm here for you and I will fight this b.s. with you." In these examples we observe how the individual poster becomes an agentive actor, that is to say, they are always involved in the action described by the verb.

The other set of verbs that are strongly present in the data analyzed are existential verbal processes, which define the existence of something or someone. In particular, the list shows the frequent use of the verb "to exist"; these verbs are mainly included in tweets that acknowledge trans people's existence in opposition to the attempt at erasing them, with posts by both trans individuals and trans allies.

3.8 Concluding Remarks

In this case study on the linguistic and discursive choices of Twitter users employing the hashtag #wontbeerased, I tried to observe the data to draw some conclusions with regard to the strategies put forward by LGBTQ+ digital activists. Some of these strategies overlap with those that had already been pointed out by other scholars, for example the use of visual and multimodal elements within the tweets, or the need to establish a connection between the online and the offline mobilization. Some other strategies seem to be peculiar to my set of data, although I wonder if more overlaps between strategies would be found if there were more studies with a linguistic perspective to compare with.

In particular, I explore four different patterns retrieved in the data. First is the practice of hashtagging, by which LGBTQ+ digital activists create meaning using hashtags. I argue that this modality of using many hashtags contemporarily can be seen as an evolution of the way in which these symbols were traditionally thought of and could be seen as a peculiarity of digital activism on social media. The second is the strong presence of multimodal elements. By multimodal elements I do not refer only to images or photos, as in the case study by Esposito and Sinatora (2021) for example, but rather to a consistent and powerful use of emojis, which serves the purpose of reinforcing the point being made while encouraging other people to take action in the fight against the marginalization of trans individuals. This agentive push that I observe in the use of multimodal elements is reinforced by the practice of direct tagging, thus of giving people a central role in this mobilization. This observation stems from an analysis of the use of the @ sign; this also highlighted the strong presence of political personalities, both taking stances in support of the trans community but also being actively involved in the tweets. Lastly, I looked at verbal processes.

Here, we see that LGBTQ+ digital activists employ a type of discourse that opposes online hate through the use of supportive and encouraging messages, making use of particular verbal processes. Although these discursive patterns might hint at a sort of "battlefield" language, the in-depth analysis reveals that the verbs are used in a positive way and the language is directed toward the production of a beneficial meaning.

The analysis of this case study demonstrates the importance and the value of LGBTQ+ digital activism in the fight for social change. First and foremost, it provides a space in which activists can feel safe to express their thoughts; secondly, it allows them to reach a much greater public that crosses national and international borders, echoing worldwide and receiving support. The #wontbeerased hashtag was launched in 2018 to counterattack one of the most violent aggressions perpetuated against the trans community at an official level, by the governing body; LGBTQ+ digital activists were able to have their voices heard, and they continue to do so through this hashtag even years later.

This case study obviously has some limitations, mainly in the fact that it only takes into account a limited number of tweets produced during a limited amount of time. Future research could enrich this case study by adding more data or looking at how other hashtags were used for similar purposes. The changes that were made to the platform now called X and formerly known as Twitter might limit this type of investigation; nonetheless, looking at different social media platforms would offer an important contribution to this area of inquiry.

4 LGBTQ+ and Feminist Digital Activism

4.1 Concluding Discussion

The rise of the Web 2.0 and of a new communicative paradigm (KhoshraviNik 2017) that fostered the rise of new linguistic strategies able to thrive in a digital environment has pushed scholars interested in the analysis of language use to try and capture the nuances of this novel communicative style. Most importantly, it has encouraged them to observe the way in which it impacts our society, which is increasingly mediated by digital technology to the point that attempts are being made to create a parallel digital universe of existence; see, for example, the ultimate work in terms of innovation technology, the metaverse,[18] a virtual reality social platform launched in 2022 by Mark Zuckerberg's enterprise. While just a few years ago this would have been considered science fiction, the reality of our society is that life is increasingly being lived digitally. This is even more so after a global pandemic spread worldwide, forcing people to

---

[18] www.wired.com/story/what-is-the-metaverse.

remain in their houses to stay alive. While individuals used to passively receive digital innovation, a number of scholars have now challenged this assumption and view people as having agency, as being active participants in the creation and development of digital environments (Androutsopoulos, 2014; Szabla and Blommaert, 2020; Tagg *et al.*, 2017). The COVID-19 pandemic also helped to speed up this process. The active role of individuals is strictly connected to the growing wave of digital activism that permeates media discourses, from #BlackLivesMatter (Nartey, 2022b) to #MeToo (Bouvier, 2020; Mendes *et al.*, 2018). New digital technologies have, in fact, helped make marginalized communities' protests and social movements visible and create networks beyond national borders and on a global scale. As Nartey (2022a:2) maintains, "digital activism and the digital environment serves as a way to center the voice and agency of minority groups, including positive self-representation and their solidarity formation for group empowerment. Social media can be used to advance the goals of repressed groups in order to instigate progressive social change." In line with this, I argue that LGBTQ+ and feminist digital activism can easily fall under the category of emancipatory discourses (Nartey, 2022a), seen as the way in which marginalized and discriminated groups have historically resisted and challenged the status quo (Lazar, 2014).

This Element sets out to open up the conversation about LGBTQ+ and feminist digital activism within the field of linguistics while trying to identify some preliminary, generalized, linguistic and discursive patterns employed to carry out mobilizations online. The discussion presented in Section 2 is meant to outline a sort of state of the art in the field, and it undoubtedly reveals a gap within the field of linguistics; most of the literature reviewed discusses the work of sociology, communication and gender studies scholars. While I value this scholarship and actively make use of the findings proposed by these colleagues, I wonder if an analysis using the tools of applied linguistics and discourse analysis could reveal even further valuable elements about the way LGBTQ+ and feminist digital activism is done, perhaps in relation to the content of the messages that these activists put forward rather than the modalities used. As a point in fact, as mentioned in Section 3.8, while some of the patterns retrieved in the #wontebeerased case study align and overlap with those discussed in the literature review, others are peculiar to this set of data. It is against this backdrop that I wonder whether offering a linguistic perspective in the analysis of digital activism movements might highlight more common patterns in the way that LGBTQ+ and feminist digital activism is done.

Contemporarily, in the attempt at delineating a possible set of patterns that could be associated in a more generalized way with the actions and words of LGBTQ+ and feminist digital activists, multimodality is one that definitely seems to be recurrent. Here, by multimodal I also mean multisemiotic; in fact, it is not only images that are often found along the sides of hashtags or other forms of digital communication for activist purposes, but also elements such as emojis or more elaborate graphicons (Herring and Daines, 2017) such as memes, alongside the use of posters and even complex products like videos or performances. Close at hand with multimodality, the use of hashtags and hashtagging also takes an unquestionable central role, to the point that digital activism comes to be known as hashtag activism as well. Hashtags not only aid in the creation and circulation of the message but also enable people to connect in the narration of shared lived experiences, emotions and actions. This last point has been identified as one of the benefits of digital activism, the possibility of identifying in other people's narratives those who have lived a similar experience and are most likely to understand the struggle. At the same time, shared narratives prove to a greater public that discriminatory and marginalizing behaviors are not isolated incidents but are, unfortunately, somewhat of a daily reality for certain groups in our society. One last element which can be counted within the great innovation of digital activism, and of digital environments in general, is that of opening up new spaces for marginalized communities to express themselves, but also a space in which it is possible to create a connection between the online and the offline experience, enabling new ways of doing activism as well as communication online.

While the research carried out for this Element allowed me to better grasp the state of digital activism both in general and with a focus on gender identity and sexuality, it still raised a number of questions that have been partially introduced throughout the previous section and by some of the scholars whose work was discussed here. These questions emerge from the reflection on the downsides of digital activism. One of these is related to the diverse accessibility of people to digital technology, which is a twofold issue. I argue that this point has two sides to it because diverse accessibility (see Section 2.1.2) can be caused either by lack of economic resources on the part of the user or the country in general, or by lack of freedom of speech. How can research in digital activism contribute to ending these types of limitations? Identifying the gaps is one step. Countries in which research in digital activism is not documented are probably those in which activism is more difficult to carry out due to the first or the second, or both, of the reasons just listed. What can be done to support activists who face these types of limitations? Perhaps highlighting countries in which difficulties emerge from lack of economic resources can initiate a chain of support and economic aid toward those parts of the world that have little access to technology or digitalization. The discourse changes drastically for those countries in which perhaps access to technology is overdeveloped but there is strict censorship; what can be done to ensure the security of digital activists? As discussed in Section 2.2.2, moving away from predetermined Western epistemologies of doing activism might be one solution, as Phillips (2014, 2020) shows through his work. But there are, unfortunately, countries in which censorship and persecution of minorities are much stricter than the reality of Singapore. For this reason and many others, these questions remain unanswered in this context.

Another issue that is most likely to remain unanswered has to do with the concept of marketization of LGBTQ+ and feminist protests. Some scholars (see, among others, Mikulak, 2019; Rice, 2023) warn the public of the possibility that marketization and monetization of these protests becomes so important that it could surpass the scope of the protest to the point that the very aim of the protest is forgotten. Can this be seen the other way around? Perhaps it is time that the linguistic community suggests some strategies that can be used to exploit the marketization of LGBTQ+ and feminist digital activism to its own benefit. Changing this perspective with effective linguistic strategies could represent a turning point for LGBTQ+ and feminist digital activism, especially in those countries or cultures in which these discourses still struggle to get through.

These are just two of the downsides of digital activism that have already been brought to the fore and that I try once again to highlight. Linguistic scholarship in this area could potentially play a role in addressing them. In fact, as Nartey (2022a:5) posits, it is our job as applied linguists and (critical) discourse analysts to "expose and resist the inequalities and injustices in society, [while adopting] an activist-scholar posture in order to push for positive social change. By so doing, our research will not only be done on social groups, but more importantly, for and with them."

4.2 On Moving the Field Forward

This Element aims at being a starting point for scholars in applied linguistics to explore LGBTQ+ and feminist digital activism further. However, the first step in this process lies in actually recognizing that a lot of the work that linguists have already been doing is focusing on LGBTQ+ and feminist digital activism, but simply not being labeled using this definition. It is time to categorize studies in LGBTQ+ and feminist digital activism as such. The first sections of this Element clearly show the abundance of the literature that looks at the use of hashtags or, more generally, language employed for the purpose of fighting discrimination. At the moment, studies that fall under this description can be found grouped by methodological approach, rather than scrutinized by platform. Grouping them under the label of LGBTQ+ and feminist digital activism could be useful not only to retrace common patterns and identify more clearly the gaps that need further investigation, but also to weave a more intricate web with other disciplines rather than simply taking from them.

Additionally, like in many other circumstances, the study of English language content prevails over other languages. While this is related to the fact that data in English is more abundant and more easily retrievable, the field could really benefit from perspectives into other idioms and cultures. This is especially so if we think of how much could be gained from this type of investigation. On the one hand, this could lead to answers to some of the questions related to downsides of digital activism that were discussed earlier; on the other, these perspectives could open up new modalities of doing digital activisms that the Western world has not yet conceptualized.

As the case study presented in Section 3 and the review of the existing scholarship in Section 2 have shown, multimodal and multisemiotic elements play a seminal role in digital activism. For this reason, another way of enhancing the field would be to focus more extensively on these elements, to explore the role of this novel way of using language and the reason why it is so prominent in online mobilization. Is it simply mirroring the way society is changing toward a more fluid way of communicating or does it contribute to digital activism in a specific and necessary way?

There are many directions in which this field can grow and expand. Here I discuss just a small illustration of them. The hope is for this Element to be the first step toward a more in-depth and extensive exploration of LGBTQ+ and feminist digital activism.

In a time (November 2022) in which Twitter, one of the most commonly used platforms for digital activism, is undergoing a radical adjustment due to its unexpected change in ownership (Clayton and Hoskins, 2022), and the rules that regulate the use of free – or otherwise known as hate (Zottola 2020b) – speech are being completely overturned, studies on the language used in LGBTQ+ and feminist digital activist are gaining a renewed importance. The linguistic patterns and discursive choices that will be used for digital activism will play, unmistakably, a crucial role in distinguishing between discrimination and the fight against it.

References

Androutsopoulos, J. (2014). Moments of sharing: Entextualization and linguistic repertoires in social networking. *Journal of Pragmatics*, *73*(Nov): 4–18.

Austin, J. L. (1962). *How to Do Things with Words*. Oxford: Clarendon.

Avineri, N., Graham, L. R., Johnson, E. J., Riner, R. C., and Rosa, J. (2018). Introduction: Reimagining language and social justice. In *Language and Social Justice in Practice*. London: Routledge, pp. 1–16.

Baer, H. (2016). Redoing feminism: Digital activism, body politics, and neoliberalism. *Feminist Media Studies*, *16*(1): 17–34.

Bailey, M. (2016). Redefining representation: Black trans and queer women's digital media production. *Screen Bodies*, *1*(1): 71–86.

Baker, P. (2023). *Using Corpora in Discourse Analysis* (second edition). London: Bloomsbury.

Baker, P, Hardie, A., and McEnery, T. (2006). *A Glossary of Corpus Linguistics*. Edinburgh: Edinburgh University Press.

Balirano, G., and Hughes, B. (2020). *Homing in on Hate: Critical Discourse Studies of Hate Speech, Discrimination and Inequality in the Digital Age*. Naples: Paolo Loffredo Editore.

Baran, D. (2022). "Rainbow plague" or "rainbow allies"? Tęcza "rainbow" as a floating signifier in the contestation of Poland's national identity. *Gender & Language*, *13*(3): 286–307.

Barker-Plummer, B., and Barker-Plummer, D. (2017). Twitter as a feminist resource: #YesAllWomen, digital platforms, and discursive social change. In *Social Movements and Media*. Bingley: Emerald Publishing Limited, pp. 91–118.

Barksdale, A. (2015). 15 tweets that flawlessly describe #GrowingUpGay, www.huffpost.com/entry/growingupgay_n_55a6b2e4e4b04740a3dec376.

Baron, A., Rayson, P., and Archer, D. (2009) Word frequency and key word statistics in historical corpus linguistics. *Anglistik: International Journal of English Studies*, *20*(1): 41–67.

Bennett, C. J., and Lyon, D. (2019). Data-driven elections: Implications and challenges for democratic societies. *Internet Policy Review*, (8)4. https://policyreview.info/pdf/policyreview-2019-4-1433.pdf.

Biber, D., and Reppen, R. (2015). *The Cambridge Handbook of English Corpus Linguistics*. Cambridge: Cambridge University Press.

Borba, R. (2022). Enregistering "Gender Ideology." *Journal of Language and Sexuality*, *11*(1): 57–79.

Breeze, R. (2011). Critical discourse analysis and its critics. *Pragmatics*, *21*(4): 493–525.

Brezhia, V. (2018). *Statistics in Corpus Linguistics. A Practical Guide.* Cambridge: Cambridge University Press.

Brindle, A. (2016). *The Language of Hate: A Corpus Linguistic Analysis of White Supremacist Language.* New York: Routledge.

Brookes, G., and McEnery, T. (2020). Corpus linguistics. In S. Adolphs and D. Knight, eds., *The Routledge Handbook of English Language and Digital Humanities.* New York: Routledge, pp. 378–404.

Burnard, L. (1999). Users reference guide for the BNC sampler. *Available on the BNC Sampler CD.* www.natcorp.ox.ac.uk/corpus/sampler.

Castillo-Esparcia, A., Caro-Castaño, L. and Almansa-Martínez, A. (2023). Evolution of digital activism on social media: opportunities and challenges. *Profesional De La información Information Professional, 32*(3): e320303. https://doi.org/10.3145/epi.2023.may.03

Cavalcante, A. (2016). "I did it all online": Transgender identity and the management of everyday life. *Critical Studies in Media Communication, 33*(1): 109–122.

Cervi, L., and Divon, T. (2023). Playful activism: Memetic performances of Palestinian resistance in TikTok #Challenges. *Social Media + Society, 9*(1). DOI: https://doi.org/10.1177/20563051231157607.

Cervi, L. and Marín-Lladó, C. (2022) Freepalestine on TikTok: from performative activism to (meaningful) playful activism, Journal of International and Intercultural Communication, *15*(4): 414–434. DOI: 10.1080/17513057 .2022.2131883

Chałupnik, M., and Brookes, G. (2022). Discursive acts of resistance: A multimodal critical discourse analysis of ALL-Poland Women's Strike's social media. *Gender and Language, 16*(3): 308–333.

Chiluwa, I. (2021). Women's online advocacy campaigns for political participation in Nigeria and Ghana. *Critical Discourse Studies, 19*(5): 465–484.

Clark, R. (2014). # NotBuyingIt: Hashtag feminists expand the commercial media conversation. *Feminist Media Studies, 14*(6): 1108–1110.

Clark, R. (2016). "Hope in a hashtag": The discursive activism of #WhyIStayed. *Feminist Media Studies, 16*(5): 788–804.

Clayton, J., and Hoskins, P. (2022). Elon Musk takes control of Twitter in $44bn deal. *BBC News.* www.bbc.com/news/technology-63402338.

Cole, K. K. (2015). "It's like she's eager to be verbally abused": Twitter, trolls, and (en)gendering disciplinary rhetoric. *Feminist Media Studies, 15*(2): 356–358.

Cullum, B. (2010). Devices: The power of mobile phones. In M. Joyce, ed., *Digital Activism Decoded: The New Mechanics of Change.* New York: International Debate Education Association, pp. 101–118.

Danesi, M. (2016). *The Semiotics of Emoji: The Rise of Visual Language in the Age of the Internet*. London: Bloomsbury.

Demata, M. (2018). "I think that maybe I wouldn't be here if it wasn't for Twitter." Donald Trump's populist style on Twitter. *Textus*, *31*(1): 67–90.

Eagle, R. B. (2015). Loitering, lingering, hashtagging: Women reclaiming public space via #BoardtheBus, #StopStreetHarassment, and the #EverydaySexism Project. *Feminist Media Studies*, *15*(2): 350–353.

Egbert, J., Biber, D., and Gray, B. (2022). *Designing and Evaluating Language Corpora: A Practical Framework for Corpus Representativeness*. Cambridge: Cambridge University Press.

Esposito, E., and Sinatora, F. L. (2021). Social media discourses of feminist protest from the Arab Levant: Digital mirroring and transregional dialogue. *Critical Discourse Studies*, *19*(5): 502–522, DOI: https://doi.org/10.1080/17405904.2021.1999291.

Esposito, E., and Zollo, S. A. (2021). "How dare you call her a pig, I know several pigs who would be upset if they knew": A multimodal critical discursive approach to online misogyny against UK MPs on YouTube. *Journal of Language Aggression and Conflict*, *9*(1): 47–75.

Evert, S. (2008). Corpora and collocations. In A. Lüdeling and M. Kytö, eds., *Corpus Linguistics: An International Handbook*. Berlin: Mouton de Gruyter, pp. 1212–1248.

Fenton, N. (2016a). *Digital, Political, Radical*. Cambridge: Polity Press.

Fenton, N. (2016b). Left out? Digital media, radical politics and social change. *Information, Communication & Society*, *19*(3): 346–361.

Finley, T. (2015). Black Twitter nailed what it was like #GrowingUpBlack. www.huffpost.com/entry/growingupblack-takes-black-twitter-down-memory-lane_n_55a675dae4b0896514cfe581.

Fischer, M. (2016). # Free_CeCe: The material convergence of social media activism. *Feminist Media Studies*, *16*(5): 755–771.

Fraser, N. (1990). Rethinking the public sphere: A contribution to the critique of actually existing democracy. *Social Text*, *25/26*: 56–80.

Fruttaldo, A. (2020). Communing affiliation and the power of bonding icons in collective narratives: The case of #GrowingUpGay. In B. Lewandoska-Tomaszczyk, V. Monello and M. Venuti, eds., *Language, Heart and Mind: Studies at the Intersection of Emotion and Cognition*. Berlin: Peter Lang, pp. 283–301.

Gal, S. (2018). Registers in circulation: The social organization of interdiscursivity. *Signs and Society*, *6*(1): 1–24.

Garside, R., and Smith, N. (1997). A hybrid grammatical tagger: CLAWS 4. In R. Garside, G. Leech and T. McEnery, eds., *Corpus Annotation:*

Linguistic Information from Computer Text Corpora. London: Longman, pp. 102–121.

Gerbaudo, P. (2017). From cyber-autonomism to cyber-populism: An ideological history of digital activism. *TripleC: Communication, Capitalism & Critique, 15*(2): 477–489.

Gillings, M., Mautner, G., and Baker, P. (2023). *Corpus-Assisted Discourse Studies*. Cambridge: Cambridge University Press.

Gounari, P. (2022). *From Twitter to Capitol Hill: Far-Right Authoritarian Populist Discourses, Social Media and Critical Pedagogy*. Leiden: Brill.

Goswami, M. P. (2018). Social media and hashtag activism. In S. Bala, M. Kaur and D. Rastogi, eds., *Liberty, Dignity and Change in Journalism*. New Delhi: Kanishka Publishers, pp. 252–262.

Habermas, J. (1962). *An Inquiry into a Category of Bourgeois Society: The Structural Transformation of the Public Sphere*. Cambridge: Polity.

Habermas, J., Lennox, S., and Lennox, F. (1974). The public sphere: An encyclopedia article (1964). *New German Critique, 3*: 49–55.

Halliday, M. A. K. (1978). *Language as social semiotic: The social interpretation of language and meaning*. London: Edward Arnold.

Hardie, A. (2012). CQPweb: Combining power, flexibility and usability in a corpus analysis tool. *International Journal of Corpus Linguistics, 17*(3): 380–409.

Hart, C., and Kelsey, D. (2022). *Discourses of Disorder*. Edinburgh: Edinburgh University Press.

Herring, S. C., and Dainas, A. R. (2017). "Nice picture comment!" Graphicons in Facebook comment threads. Paper presented at the proceedings of the 50th Hawaii International Conference on System Sciences, Hilton Waikoloa Village, HI, 4–7 January.

Heuer, G., and Macomber, M. (2022). Gender and Instagram activism in teenagers: Social discourse in a digital age. *Journal of Student Research, 11* (3). DOI:https://doi.org/10.47611/jsrhs.v11i3.2918.

Horeck, T. (2014). #AskThicke: "Blurred Lines," rape culture, and the feminist hashtag takeover. *Feminist Media Studies, 14*(6): 1105–1107.

Hundley, H. L., and Rodriguez, J. S. (2009). Transactivism and postmodernity: An agonistic analysis of transliterature. *Communication Quarterly, 57*(1): 35–50.

Hunston, S. (2002). *Corpora in Applied Linguistics*. Cambridge: Cambridge University Press.

Inclán, M. (2018). *The Zapatista Movement and Mexico's Democratic Transition: Mobilization, Success, and Survival*. New York: Oxford Scholarship Online.

Jackson, S. J. (2016). (Re) imagining intersectional democracy from Black feminism to hashtag activism. *Women's Studies in Communication, 39*(4): 375–379.

Jackson, S. J. (2018). Progressive social movements and the internet. In D. Cloud, ed., *Oxford Encyclopedia of Communication and Critical Studies*. Oxford: Oxford University Press. DOI:https://doi.org/10.1093/acre fore/9780190228613.013.644.

Jackson, S. J., Bailey, M., and Foucault Welles, B. (2018). #GirlsLikeUs: Trans advocacy and community building online. *New Media & Society, 20*(5): 1868–1888.

Jackson, S. J., Bailey, M., and Welles, B. F. (2020). *#HashtagActivism: Networks of race and gender justice*. Cambridge: Massachusetts Institute of Technology Press.

Jackson, S., Bailey, M., and Foucault Welles, B. (2019). Women tweet on violence: From #YesAllWomen to #MeToo. *Ada: A Journal of Gender, New Media, and Technology*, (15). DOI: https://doi.org/10.5399/uo/ada.2019.15.6.

Jenzen, O., and Lewin, T. (2021). LGBTQ+ visual activism. In D. Lilleker and A. Veneti, eds., *The Research Handbook in Visual Politics*. Cheltenham: Edward Elgar, pp. 284–297.

Jones, L., Chałupnik, M., Mackenzie, J., and Mullany, L. (2022). "STFU and start listening to how scared we are": Resisting misogyny on Twitter via #NotAllMen. *Discourse, Context & Media, 47*: 100596.

Jouët, J. (2018). Digital feminism: Questioning the renewal of activism. *Journal of Research in Gender Studies, 8*(1), 133–157.

Joyce, M. C. (2010). *Digital Activism Decoded: The New Mechanics of Change*. New York: IDEA.

Karatzogianni, A. (2015). *Firebrand Waves of Digital Activism 1994–2014: The Rise and Spread of Hacktivism and Cyberconflict*. Bern: Springer.

Katz, J. K., and Crocker, E. L. (2015). Selfies and photo messaging as visual conversation: Reports from the United States, United Kingdom and China. *International Journal of Communication*, 2015: 2387–2396.

Kaun, A., and Treré, E. (2020). Repression, resistance and lifestyle: Charting (dis)connection and activism in times of accelerated capitalism. *Social Movement Studies, 19*(5–6): 697–715.

Kaun, A., and Uldam, J. (2018). Digital activism: After the hype. *New Media & Society, 20*(6): 2099–2106.

Khoja-Moolji, S. (2015). Becoming an "intimate public": Exploring the affective intensities of hashtag feminism. *Feminist Media Studies, 15*(2): 347–350.

KhosraviNik, M. (2017). Social media critical discourse studies (SM-CDS). In J. Flowerdew and J. E. Richardson, eds., *The Routledge Handbook of Critical Discourse Studies*. London: Routledge, pp. 582–596.

KhosraviNik, M. (2022). Digital meaning-making across content and practice in social media critical discourse studies, *Critical Discourse Studies, 19*(2): 119–123.

KhoshraviNik, M. (2023). *Social Media Critical Discourse Studies*. London: Routledge.

KhoshraviNik, M., and Esposito, E. (2018). Online hate, digital discourse and critique: Exploring digitally-mediated discursive practices of gender-based hostility. *Lodz Papers in Pragmatics*, *14*(1): 45–68.

Kim, J. (2017). # iamafeminist as the "mother tag": Feminist identification and activism against misogyny on Twitter in South Korea. *Feminist Media Studies*, *17*(5): 804–820.

Knight, D. (2015). e-Language: Communication in the Digital Age. In P. Baker and T. McEnery, eds., *Corpora and Discourse Studies: Integrating Discourse and Corpora*. Basingstoke: Palgrave MacMillan, pp. 20–40.

Koester, A. (2022). Building small specialised corpora. In A. O'Keeffe and M. McCarthy, eds., *The Routledge Handbook of Corpus Linguistics* (second edition). Oxon: Routledge, pp. 48–61.

Kopytowska, M. (2017). Discourses of hate and radicalism in action. In M. Kopytowska, ed., *Contemporary Discourses of Hate and Radicalism across Space and Genres*. Amsterdam: John Benjamins, pp. 1–12.

Laclau, E. (2005). *On Populist Reason*. London: Verso.

Lagerkvist, A. (2019). *Digital Existence: Ontology, Ethics and Transcendence in Digital Culture*. London: Routledge.

Larrondo, A., Morales i Gras, J. and Orbegozo Terradillos, J. (2019). Feminist hashtag activism in Spain: Measuring the degree of politicisation of online discourse on #YoSíTeCreo, #HermanaYoSíTeCreo, #Cuéntaloy #NoEstásSola. *Communication & Society*, *32*(4): 207–221.

Latina, D., and Docherty, S. (2014). Trending participation, trending exclusion? *Feminist Media Studies*, *14*(6): 1103–1105.

Lazar, M. (2014). Feminist critical discourse analysis relevance for current gender and language research. In S. Ehrlich, M. Meyerhoff and J. Holmes, eds., *The Handbook of Language, Gender, and Sexuality*. New York: John Wiley & Sons, pp. 180–199.

Logi, L., and Zappavigna, M. (2021). A social semiotic perspective on emoji: How emoji and language interact to make meaning in digital messages. *New Media & Society*, 25(1): 3222–3246.

Losh, E. (2014). Hashtag feminism and Twitter activism in India. *Social Epistemology Review and Reply Collective*, *3*(3): 11–22.

Loza, S. (2014). Hashtag feminism,# SolidarityIsForWhiteWomen, and the other #FemFuture. *Ada: A Journal of Gender, New Media, and Technology*, (5): *Queer Feminist Media Praxis (July 2014)*.

Mann, A. (2014). *Global Activism in Food Politics: Power Shift*. Bern: Springer.

Mendes, K., Ringrose, J. and Keller, J. (2018). #MeToo and the promise and pitfalls of challenging rape culture through digital feminist activism. *European Journal of Women's Studies, 25*(2): 236–246.

Meyer, M. D. (2014). #Thevagenda's war on headlines: Feminist activism in the information age. *Feminist Media Studies, 14*(6): 1107–1108.

Mikulak, M. (2019). Between the market and the hard place: Neoliberalization and the Polish LGBT movement, *Social Movement Studies, 18*(5): 550–565.

Milan, S., and Van-der-Velden, L. (2016). The alternative epistemologies of data activism. *Digital Culture & Society, 2*(2): 57–74.

Mossberger, K., Tolbert, C. J. and McNeal, R. S. (2007). *Digital Citizenship: The Internet, Society, and Participation.* Cambridge: Massachusetts Institute of Technology Press.

Myers, R. (2019). The "warspeak" permeating everyday language puts us all in the trenches. *The Conversation.* Last accessed May 21, 2022, at https://theconversation.com/the-warspeak-permeating-everyday-language-puts-us-all-in-the-trenches-121356.

Nartey, M. (Ed.). (2023). *Voice, Agency and Resistance: Emancipatory Discourses in Action.* London: Routledge.

Nartey, M. (2022a). Investigating emancipatory discourses in action: The need for an interventionist approach and an activist-scholar posture. *Critical Discourse Studies, 19*(5): 459–464.

Nartey, M. (2022b). Centering marginalized voices: A discourse analytic study of the Black Lives Matter movement on Twitter. *Critical Discourse Studies, 19*(5): 523–583.

Núñez Puente, S. (2011). Feminist cyberactivism: Violence against women, internet politics, and Spanish feminist praxis online. *Continuum: Journal of Media & Cultural Studies, 25*(03): 333–346.

Ohler, J. B. (2010). *Digital Community, Digital Citizen.* Thousand Oaks: Sage.

Özkula, S. M. (2021). What is digital activism anyway? Social constructions of the "digital" in contemporary activism. *Journal of Digital Social Research, 3* (3): 60–84.

Onanuga, P. A. (2023). Weaponising digital architecture: Queer Nigerian Instagram users and digital visual activism. In D. Woodman, ed., *LGBT+ Communities – Creating Spaces of Identity.* IntechOpen. DOI: 10.5772/intechopen.108760.

Papacharissi, Z. (2014). Uses and gratifications. In *An Integrated Approach to Communication Theory and Research.* London: Routledge, pp. 151–166.

Papacharissi, Z. (2016). Affective publics and structures of storytelling: Sentiment, events and mediality. *Information, Communication & Society, 19*(3): 307–324.

Partington, A., Duguid, A., and Taylor, C. (2013). *Patterns and Meanings in Discourse*: *Theory and Practice in Corpus-Assisted Discourse Studies* (CADS). London: John Benjamins.

Phillips, R. (2020). *Virtual Activisms: Sexuality, the Internet, and a Social Movement in Singapore*. Toronto: University of Toronto Press.

Phillips, R. (2014). "And I am also gay": Illiberal pragmatics, neoliberal homonormativity and LGBT activism in Singapore. *Anthropologica*, *56*(1): 45–54.

Rasulo, M. (2023). *Master Narratives of Hate Speech: A Multimodal Analysis*. Naples: Paolo Loffedo Editore.

Rawson, K. J. (2014). Transgender worldmaking in cyberspace: Historical activism on the internet. *QED*: *A Journal in GLBTQ Worldmaking*, *1*(2): 38–60.

Rayson, P. (2009). Wmatrix: A web-based corpus processing environment. Computing Department, Lancaster University.

Raun, T. (2010). Screen-births: Exploring the transformative potential in trans video blogs on YouTube. *Graduate Journal of Social Science*, *7*(2): 113–130.

Rentschler, C. (2015). # Safetytipsforladies: Feminist Twitter takedowns of victim blaming. *Feminist Media Studies*, *15*(2): 353–356.

Rice, J. (2023). Rainbow-washing. *Northeastern University Law Review*, *15*(2): 285–358.

Riboni, G. (2020). *Discourses of Authenticity on YouTube. From Personal to the Professional*. Milan: Edizioni Universitarie di Lettere Economia Diritto.

Szabla, M., and Blommaert, J. (2020). Does context really collapse in social media interaction? *Applied Linguistic Review*, *11*(2): 251–279.

Scholz, T. (2010). Infrastructure: Its transformations and effect on digital activism. In M. C. Joyce, ed., *Digital Activism Decoded: The New Mechanics of Change*. New York: International Debate Education Association, pp. 17–32.

Schultz, D., and Jungherr, A. (2010). Picking the right one in a transient world. In M. C. Joyce, ed., *Digital Activism Decoded: The New Mechanics of Change*. Utrecht: International Debate Education Association, pp. 33–45.

Searle, J. R. (1969). *Speech Acts*. Cambridge: Cambridge University Press.

Searle, J. R. (1976). A classification of illocutionary acts. *Language in Society*, *5*(1): 1–23.

Squires, C. R. (2016). *Dangerous Discourses: Feminism, Gun Violence and Civic Life*. Berlin: Peter Lang Publishing.

Stenglin, M. (2011). Interpersonal meaning in 3D spaces: How bonding icon gets its "charge." In L. Unsworth, ed., *Multimodal Semiotics: Functional Analysis in Contexts of Education*. London: Continuum, pp. 50–66.

Tagg, C., Seargeant, P. and Brown, A. (2017). *Taking Offence on Social Media: Conviviality and Communication on Facebook*. London: Palgrave Macmillan.

Tazi, M., and Oumlil, K. (2020). The rise of fourth-wave feminism in the Arab region? Cyberfeminism and women's activism at the crossroads of the Arab Spring. *CyberOrient*, *14*(1): 44–71.

Tortajada, I., Willem, C. R., Platero Méndez, L., and Araüna, N. (2021). *Lost in Transition?* Digital trans activism on Youtube. *Information, Communication & Society*, *24*(8): 1091–1107.

Vie, S. (2014). In defense of "slacktivism": The Human Rights Campaign Facebook logo as digital activism. *First Monday*, *19*(4). DOI: https://doi.org/10.5210/fm.v19i4.4961.

Webster, K. (2022). A textual analysis of online asexual representation and visibility on Reddit. In J. H. Lipschultz, K. Freberg and R. Luttrell, eds., *The Emerald Handbook of Computer-Mediated Communication and Social Media*. Leeds: Emerald Publishing Limited, pp. 177–195.

Williams, S. (2015). Digital defense: Black feminists resist violence with hashtag activism. *Feminist Media Studies*, *15*(2): 341–344.

Wilson, A., and Rayson, P. (1993). Automatic content analysis of spoken discourse: A report on work in progress. In C. Souter and E. Atwell, eds., *Corpus Based Computational Linguistics*. Amsterdam: Rodopi, pp. 215–226.

Xie, C., and Yus, F. (2021). Digitally mediated communication. In M. Haugh, D. Kádár and M. Terkourafi, eds., *The Cambridge Handbook of Sociopragmatics* (Cambridge Handbooks in Language and Linguistics). Cambridge: Cambridge University Press, pp. 454–474.

Yamamura, S. (2022). Impact of COVID-19 pandemic on the transnationalization of LGBT* activism in Japan and beyond. *Global Networks*, *2023*(23): 120–131.

Yates, S. J. (1996). Oral and written linguistic aspects of computer conferencing. *Pragmatics and Beyond New Series*, *39*: 29–46.

Zappavigna, M. (2012). *Discourse of Twitter and Social Media: How We Use Language to Create Affiliation on the Web*. London: Bloomsbury.

Zappavigna, M. (2018). *Searchable Talk: Hashtags and Social Media Metadiscourse*. London: Bloomsbury.

Zottola, A. (2021). *Transgender Identities in the Press: A Corpus-Based Discourse Analysis*. London: Bloomsbury.

Zottola, A. (2020a). Corpus linguistics and digital humanities: Intersecting paths. A case study from Twitter. *América Critica*, *4*(2): 131–141.

Zottola, A. (2020b). When freedom of speech turns into freedom to hate. Hateful speech and 'othering' in conservative political propaganda in the USA. In G. Balirano and B. Hughes, eds., *Homing in on Hate: Critical Discourse Studies of Hate Speech, Discrimination and Inequality in the Digital Age*. Naples: Paolo Loffredo Editore, pp. 93–112.

To Dario

Cambridge Elements ☰

Language, Gender and Sexuality

Helen Sauntson

York St John University

Helen Sauntson is Professor of English Language and Linguistics at York St John University, UK. Her research areas are language in education and language, gender and sexuality. She is co-editor of *The Palgrave Studies in Language, Gender and Sexuality* book series, and she sits on the editorial boards of the journals *Gender and Language* and the *Journal of Language and Sexuality*. Within her institution, Helen is Director of the Centre for Language and Social Justice Research.

Holly R. Cashman

University of New Hampshire

Holly R. Cashman is Professor of Spanish at University of New Hampshire (USA), core faculty in Women's and Gender Studies, and coordinator of Queer Studies. She is past president of the International Gender and Language Association (IGALA) and of the executive board of the Association of Language Departments (ALD) of the Modern Languages Association. Her research interests include queer(ing) multilingualism and language, gender, and sexuality.

Editorial Board

About the Series

Cambridge Elements in Language, Gender and Sexuality highlights the role of language in understanding issues, identities and relationships in relation to multiple genders and sexualities. The series provides a comprehensive home for key topics in the field which readers can consult for up-to-date coverage and the latest developments.

Cambridge Elements ≡

Language, Gender and Sexuality

Elements in the Series

The Language of Gender-Based Separatism
Veronika Koller, Alexandra Krendel, and Jessica Aiston

Queering Sexual Health Translation Pedagogy
Piero Toto

Legal Categorization of "Transgender": An Analysis of Statutory Interpretation of "Sex", "Man", and "Woman" in Transgender Jurisprudence
Kimberly Tao

LGBTQ+ and Feminist Digital Activism: A Linguistic Perspective
Angela Zottola

Printed in the United States
by Baker & Taylor Publisher Services